AUSTRALIAN ENCOUNTERS

Published by Black Inc.,
an imprint of Schwartz Media Pty Ltd
37–39 Langridge Street
Collingwood VIC 3066 Australia
email: enquiries@blackincbooks.com
http://www.blackincbooks.com

The National Library of Australia Cataloguing-in-Publication entry:

     Maloney, Shane.

     Australian encounters / Shane Maloney ;
     illustrated by Chris Grosz.

     ISBN: 9781863955058 (hbk.)

     Celebrities--Biography.

     Other Authors/Contributors: Grosz, Chris.

     920.02

Book design: Thomas Deverall
Printed and bound in China by Imago

For digital prints of illustrations, contact chris@chrisgrosz.com

CONTENTS

INTRODUCTION

CHRIS GROSZ AND I ARE DELIGHTED TO PRESENT THIS COLLECTION OF memorable meetings, all but one of which first appeared in the *Monthly* magazine. Chris paints the pictures, I write the words.

All of the encounters depicted in this book really happened. None is concocted, fabricated or invented. Each is described as accurately as the available information permits and our creative abilities allow.

They were inspired by a series of vignettes which appeared in the *Atlantic* magazine during the 1980s. Written and illustrated by Edward and Nancy Sorel, these 'First Encounters' depicted personal convergences of world significance, quirky episodes of happenstance and truly odd interactions, all of them true. They were informative, astringent and often astonishing. I resolved to abduct the concept at the first opportunity and produce an Australian equivalent.

That opportunity arose in 2005 when the *Monthly* expressed an interest in the idea. I immediately set about finding a collaborator, preferably someone who had a box of colouring pencils and an eye for esoteric couplings. Chris Grosz possessed both. A long-time Australian resident who had recently returned to his native New Zealand, he also enjoyed the advantage of being 2600 kilometres away.

Our first 'Encounter' was George Johnston and Leonard Cohen. It established the template for all the encounters that followed.

First, at least one of the individuals must be a prominent Australian, or at least identified as a figure in Australian history.

Second, the interactions and their circumstances must be verifiable from published sources. If living, efforts should be made to interview the subjects. Even Brian Burke. But not Bob Hawke because you have to draw the line somewhere. Or Conrad Black because he's in gaol. Or Kylie Minogue because we're too shy. Or Faith Bandler because she's really old and we didn't want to be a nuisance and, anyway, her reminiscences are in the National Library oral history collection. Or Len Cohen or Henry Kissinger. But you get the drift. As a rule of thumb, we go for dead people. The point being, verity is our watchword.

Third, encounters need not be strictly limited to two human individuals. Space stations, warships, sheep and viruses also qualify. It depends how desperate we get.

In the process of writing and illustrating these encounters, we have learned a lot about Australian history. We didn't know much when we started, so it's been a real education. Daisy Bates and Breaker Morant were married. How amazing is that?

As to sources, the *Australian Dictionary of Biography* is an absolute treasure trove. As to meticulousness, professional nitpickers at the *Monthly* run their fine-toothed combs through our facts. Any errors are entirely the fault of Chris Grosz.

Mark Twain described Australia's history as reading like the most beautiful of lies. He didn't know the half of it. Nor did he meet anyone notable, so he's not in this book. Notwithstanding that fact, please enjoy.
                                                                    —*Shane Maloney*

Australian Encounters

On a wet March afternoon in 1960 an unknown 25-year-old Canadian poet was wandering the streets of London. Since his arrival three months earlier he'd bought himself a blue Burberry raincoat, an Olivetti typewriter and completed an autobiographical novel. Now it was time to find somewhere warm to relax, drink and meet women. Somewhere cheap. Noticing a Bank of Greece sign, he stepped inside and saw a teller with a deep tan and sunglasses. Within a few days Leonard Cohen was boarding a steamer in Piraeus for the five-hour trip to Hydra.

What he found was a cluster of whitewashed houses arrayed around a small horseshoe-shaped harbour. Many of the houses were uninhabited and there were no cars or trucks, few telephones, limited electricity and, despite the name, little fresh water. At the end of the cobbled waterfront stood the Katsikas brothers' grocery store. In its backroom bar, amid tins of olive oil and sacks of flour, he met an Australian expatriate named George Johnston.

It was five years since Johnston and his writer wife Charmian Clift had settled on Hydra, trading the security of a newspaper career for the vagaries of a literary life. Things were not going well. At 48, Johnston's glory days as a war correspondent and foreign editor were behind him and *My Brother Jack* was in difficult gestation. He was ill, impoverished, impotent and battling to eke a living from his work. But as presiding spirit of the island's shifting cast of foreign artists and writers, he was nothing if not hospitable.

George and Charmian put young Len up in their spare room and George arranged for him to perform some of his songs for the cosmopolitan assortment of authors, painters and musicians who frequented the Katsikas grocery, a group that included Marianne Jensen, wife of a Norwegian novelist. To Cohen, raised in an affluent Jewish family in suburban Montreal, his Australian hosts had a larger-than-life, mythical quality. "They drank more than other people, they wrote more, they got sick more, they got well more, they cursed more and they blessed more, and they helped a great deal more. They were an inspiration."

When Cohen decided to stay on Hydra and set up house for himself, they contributed a bed and a work table. And in a way, perhaps, they had also introduced him to his muse. That's her, Marianne, sitting at the table with the typewriter on the back cover of his 1969 album *Songs from a Room*. By then Cohen was the high priest of pathos, the bird on the wire, the dirge-master general. Charmian had taken her own life. And tuberculosis, cigarettes and booze would soon do the deed for George.

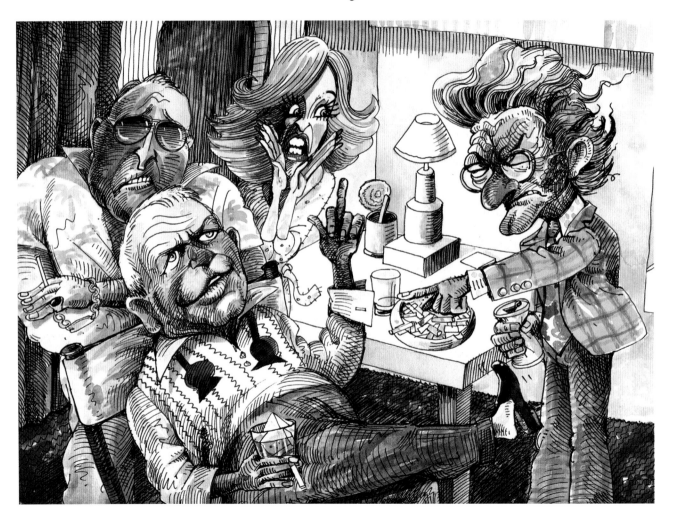

"A FUNNY THING HAPPENED IN AUSTRALIA," Frank Sinatra told a New York audience. "I made a mistake and got off the plane."

The plane in question – the private jet of one of Sinatra's Las Vegas casino connections – landed in Melbourne on 9 July 1974. Fresh out of self-imposed retirement, the 58-year-old Sinatra was visiting Australia for the first time in 15 years. His career was back on the upswing after a decade of poor record sales and crappy movies; his five shows, billed as the 'Ol' Blue Eyes Is Back' tour, were eagerly awaited.

Trouble began the moment he set foot on the ground. Nobody was waiting to pick him up. As he headed to his rehearsal in a borrowed car, he was pursued by a journalist disguised as his then wife, the former Mrs Zeppo Marx. Sprinting through the rain to the venue with a media posse at his heels, he found himself locked out. Photos splashed across the afternoon papers showed a very cranky Frankie pounding on the stage door "like a demented fan".

That night on stage, the Chairman of the Board let fly. In a prickly monologue, he described journalists as bums and "the broads who work for the press" as hookers worth "a buck and a half". The crooner had bitten off more than he could chew.

When the journalists' union demand for an apology was brushed aside, the ACTU slapped a ban on the tour. Its president, Bob Hawke, took personal charge of the campaign. The Silver Bodgie was then 45, a champion pisspot, notorious womaniser and the artful manager of Labor's industrial wing. He declared that unless Sinatra could walk on water, he would be stuck in Australia until he said sorry.

With transport workers refusing to refuel his jet, Sinatra was forced to sneak onto a commercial flight to Sydney. Holed up in the Boulevard Hotel, he considered calling on the US Navy to rescue him. Eventually, he agreed to negotiate.

On 11 July, the two men met in Sinatra's suite. Over four hours, an agreement was hammered out. In return for a statement that Sinatra "did not intend any general reflection upon the moral character of working members of the Australian media", Hawke was prepared to green-light his remaining concerts.

Back in the US, it was joked that Sinatra was only allowed out of Australia because the union boss woke one morning with a kangaroo's head on his pillow.

Hawkie, meanwhile, did it his way. Eschewing the booze and broads, he became Labor's longest-serving prime minister, until upstaged by Placido Domingo.

I T WAS GREAT WHILE IT LASTED, ACCORDING to Kylie. "I learnt a lot."

They met at a bash after the *Countdown* Awards, the program's final show, in July 1987. He was brooding, lascivious and charismatic, the rock-god frontman of INXS, a band whose name said it all. She was eight years younger, a girl-next-door soapie starlet whose pop debut, a bop-along cover version, had unexpectedly topped the charts.

Michael Hutchence had a bad-boy reputation and a widely reported taste for supermodels. Kylie Minogue had a steady boyfriend in Jason Donovan, her small-screen love interest.

When Kylie arrived, Hutchence was holding court, joking and drinking with his entourage. She'd been invited as a courtesy, and was a bit out of her depth, wide-eyed among the rock stars. Accounts differ, memories have blurred and nobody was taking notes. Some say Hutchence was drunk, others that he was just jesting. Whatever the case, neither party ever confirmed what he did the moment he noticed her.

Legend, however, is quite specific. And witnesses, speaking on condition of anonymity, confirm it. Michael jumped from his seat and flung himself towards Kylie, declaring for all to hear that he wanted to fuck her. The 20-year-old was startled. But before she had time to react, Hutchence smiled at her, spoke softly and slipped back into the crowd.

"I thoroughly enjoyed the *Countdown* Awards," Kylie told an interviewer. "I was worried that a lot of big-time rock-music people would look down on me. But they were all really nice. Michael Hutchence made an effort to come over and say hi, which was nice of him."

A year later, Hutchence was nice again. When he spotted Kylie and Jason at an INXS show, he invited them to kick on back at the band's hotel. By then, 'I Should Be So Lucky' had launched Minogue's musical career into the stratosphere. While minions plied Jason with pot, Hutchence cornered Kylie and the two spent the evening sitting on his bed, heads together, whispering and laughing.

Another year passed. Kylie quit *Neighbours* to pump out million-selling chartbusters, vapid off-the-shelf Stock Aitken Waterman dance tracks made bearable only by her cute exuberance. In August 1989, about to commence her first international tour, 'Disco in Dream', she took a short break in Hong Kong.

Hutchence, as it happened, kept an apartment there. The moment Kylie hit town, he was knocking at her door, charm itself, offering his services. Next thing, poor Jase was getting the flick.

By the time the two-year affair ended, it had transformed a singing budgie into a sex vixen and set Kylie's course towards pop divadom. It didn't do Michael Hutchence any harm, either. But he didn't need anybody's help in that regard.

ROBERT MENZIES' FIRST TRIP TO ENGLAND was a profoundly emotional experience. At 41, Jeparit-born Bob had finally come 'home'. It was 1935, the Silver Jubilee of George V, and pilgrims from the Empire were converging on London for the pomp and circumstance.

For Menzies, it was a happy convergence for a number of reasons. As the attorney-general and a member of Prime Minister Joe Lyons' entourage, he could contribute to negotiations with British trade officials. And as a barrister in private practice, he could appear for a client, Paper Sacks Pty Ltd, in its appeal to the Privy Council.

But above all, the Anglophile colonial could drink deep from the nurturing fount of English tradition and culture. There were silk knee breeches and cocked hats to be worn, Buckingham Palace and Gray's Inn to be visited. In the green and pleasant landscape, Ming discovered "the secret springs of English poetry". One Saturday afternoon in Kent, he paid a call on Winston Churchill.

For Churchill, these were the wilderness years. Past 60, politically isolated and living beyond his means, he was at his nadir. When not thundering in the House of Commons against Indian self-rule, he retreated to his country house, Chartwell, to write, paint and indulge in a little light bricklaying.

Menzies was received courteously by Mrs Churchill. Winston was in the swimming pool, Clementine explained. "It was a splendid sight," Menzies recalled in his memoir, *Afternoon Light*. The pool was large, circular and heated, and sited on a grassy slope with panoramic views. In the middle was "a jutting form rather reminiscent of the Rock of Gibraltar". The rock stirred, removed the cotton wool from its ears and waded ashore.

Tea was served and Bob listened, unimpressed, while Churchill banged on about the menace of Hitler. His host was a remarkable man, Menzies concluded, but he had a one-track mind and lacked discipline. This opinion was reinforced shortly after, when he observed Churchill in the House of Commons. "Feet of clay," he recorded in his diary.

Six years later, now the prime minister of Australia, Menzies was back in England. In response to Menzies' warnings about Japan, Churchill, now the prime minister of Great Britain, offered nothing but "blood, toil, tears and sweat".

For all his imperial rhetoric, Winnie had little interest in the dominions, much less the views of their politicians. His opinion of Menzies is nowhere recorded. But in one sense at least, Bob was his enthusiastic follower. On Sir Winston's death, Sir Robert succeeded him as the Lord Warden of the Cinque Ports.

O*H ERROL, SANG AUSTRALIAN CRAWL IN* their hymn to Tasmania's gift to swashbuckling, *I would give everything just to be like him.* Such was the strength of the Flynn legend that the band named its second album, *Sirocco*, after the schooner the adventure-seeking 20-year-old sailed from Sydney to New Guinea in 1929. Presumably it wasn't Errol the tobacco planter and slave trader that inspired the would-be bad-boys but Errol the dashing babe-magnet star of *Captain Blood*, *Mutiny on the Bounty* and *The Sea Hawk*.

But 30 years of booze, broads, green tights and frigging in the rigging are bound to take their toll, even for a leading man of Flynn's prodigious athleticism. By 1958, Hollywood's most notorious philanderer was washed up. An endless parade of box-office flops, lawsuits, unproven rape charges, drunken brawls, alimony disputes and prying tabloids sent him hunting for somewhere to "drown the pains of the world in a few daiquiris". He found it, temporarily, in Cuba.

He arrived in Havana just as Fidel Castro's rebel forces were sweeping down from the Sierra Maestra to topple the corrupt Batista dictatorship. After sampling the fleshpots, he set out to report the revolution for the Hearst press. Soon in the thick of things, he was nicked in the leg during fighting at a sugar mill, either by a bullet or a chunk of plaster – he wasn't sure which.

Two years earlier Castro had returned from exile on the yacht *Granma* to strike the spark of insurrection. Of the 80-odd rebels who sailed with him, only 12 survived. They fled to the mountains where, aided by the combat squad of Celia Sánchez, the small band swelled to hundreds, then thousands.

Now poised to take power, the 32-year-old, media-savvy Castro invited Flynn to his headquarters. "He was in the fighting zone as a kind of war correspondent," Fidel told the *LA Times*. Flynn was presented with a black kerchief and introduced to Che Guevara. Che had seen some of Flynn's films but failed to recognise Robin Hood in the bloated roué across the table. In his subsequent report Flynn described Castro's fellow revolutionary Celia Sánchez simply as "36-24-35".

Flynn thought Castro "a real man" but he preferred his revolutions at a distance and his guerrilla women on celluloid. Back in the US, he made *Attack of the Cuban Rebel Girls*, co-starring his 17-year-old girlfriend and cut around documentary footage. Too ludicrous to be called tragic, it was his last film. He died a few months later, of everything.

BOTH WERE PRINCES IN THEIR OWN LANDS. One was a scion of the squattocracy, the only son of a wealthy grazier and the grandson of a conservative politician, educated at Melbourne Grammar and Oxford University and sent to parliament at 25. Patrician in bearing and speech, he was now 48 and prime minister of Australia.

The other was one of the many children of Mungurrawuy of the Gumatj clan of the Yolngu people of Yirrkala. Raised among his siblings, then sent to Bible college in Brisbane, he was skilled in painting, dancing, acting and music. At 30 he was a seasoned interpreter and negotiator who represented 81 Aboriginal communities as the elected Chairman of the Northern Land Council.

The year was 1978 and the two men faced each other across a divide that went to the heart of their respective views of the world. For Galarrwuy Yunupingu, it was the survival of his country. For Malcolm Fraser, it was the economic development of the nation. The issue was approval of the Ranger uranium mine in Kakadu. At stake was the future of land rights legislation.

With negotiations at an impasse, Yunupingu proposed a fishing trip. Fraser, a keen angler, rose to the bait.

The place was a mangrove-fringed billabong where the creeks that flow from the Arnhem Land escarpment feed the headwaters of the South Alligator River. Mt Brockman, the site of the proposed mine, was just a few kilometres away. "I deliberately took him there so I could ask him on the spot: how could mining take place in a national park?" As they cast their lures, Yunupingu put his question.

The barramundi were biting, but Fraser wasn't. "It was an enjoyable occasion," he recalls. "I didn't feel put upon."

The PM caught ten or so nice big ones – "enough for the pot" – and there was fishing talk over dinner later in Darwin. But it was clear to Yunupingu that mining would proceed whether the Aborigines agreed or not. Later that year, under ruthless pressure from the federal government, he signed the deal.

In the years that followed, Malcolm Fraser was spurned by his own tribe and condemned to preach in the wilderness. Galarrwuy Yunupingu continues to fish in the lands of his ancestors, a perennial media target. At the Ranger mine, more than 120 incidents, spills and leaks have been reported. And as the spot price for uranium reaches a new high, the timetable for ore processing has been extended.

H E WAS A HOT-SHOT STOCK-CAR DRIVER. She was a winsome 22-year-old brain surgeon. Theirs was truly a marriage made in make-believe.

The film was released as *Days of Thunder*, but when she got the call that he wanted her to read for a part, the working title was *Daytona*, a reference to its Florida racetrack setting.

At that point, Thomas Cruise Mapother IV was one of the biggest money-spinners in Hollywood, an Oscar nominee who'd recently been voted Best Dressed Male Movie Star. Nicole Kidman, who had just made her US debut in *Dead Calm*, was sceptical but game. "I'd been to LA before. But hey, free trip!"

The reading took place in a Paramount conference room before Cruise and a small platoon of co-producers. Kidman summoned her professional nonchalance and Cruise greeted her with collegial compliments, but there was one small, unforeseen problem. The fastest rising star in show business was so short that the pilot he played in *Top Gun* would not have met the minimum height requirement for the US Navy. When he stood to shake the willowy redhead's hand, she found herself looking downwards.

Kidman knew the rules. "It simply wouldn't do, having the girlfriend tower over the macho race-car driver."

For a moment, nobody spoke. Then the two actors burst out laughing. She picked up the script and began to read. He talked intensely and did things with his hands. It was lust at first sight. Nic thought Tom was the sexiest man she'd ever clapped eyes on. Tom felt the same. "It was totally physical."

The next day she was told that she had the part. It wasn't written yet, but it was hers.

The movie was a dumb, noisy star vehicle with Cruise in almost every scene. While tropical storms lashed the racetrack set, Kidman did a lot of waiting around for her turn as the improbable eye-candy, love-interest neurosurgeon. But before the shoot was over, the two were an item.

The rest is tabloid history. For ten years, the sun shone on stardom's golden couple. He told the world to show him the money. She was to die for. Then the squirt did the dirty.

Since their divorce, Kidman has won an Oscar, sung on a hit single and dusted off her high heels. Mapother, now rich beyond the dreams of avarice, has become an Operating Thetan Seven of the inner circle. His height remains 170 centimetres.

WHEN MARGARET COURT WALKED INTO the locker room at the close of the 1973 French Open, Martina Navratilova tried not to gawk. Court was a figure of awe, the most successful player in the history of women's tennis. Navratilova was an ungainly teenager competing in her first international tournament. When the player known as 'the Arm' said hello, young Martina was "thrilled" to have been recognised. Margaret knew class when she saw it, acknowledging Navratilova as "the wave of the future".

In due course, the up-and-comer and the champ faced each other across the net. It was the quarterfinals of the 1975 Australian Open and Court was nearing the end of her stellar career. The first Australian woman to win Wimbledon, she'd taken every possible grand-slam title – singles, doubles and mixed doubles – winning at least one of these at each of the four majors. Along the way, she'd had two children and become the first mother to be world number one. At 32, she had nothing left to prove.

Eighteen-year-old Navratilova was making her Australian debut. "A bumpkin from a communist country", the eighth seed was no longer tied to the Czech tennis federation; if she didn't win enough prize money to buy a ticket to her next match in America, she'd be finished.

Instead of the main arena at Kooyong, the women were relegated to an outside court, where they were forced to play amid blaring loudspeakers and the rattle of passing trains.

Left-handed Navaratilova played better than she ever had in her life. "I took it to another level … I gave her what she didn't like: I gave her junk." She won 6–4 6–3. The win netted her $1500 but the *Sun* got her name wrong in its report the next morning.

In their bout at Wimbledon that same year, the self-described "tomboy from Albury" had her revenge, playing with "matronly dignity" to overawe and outmanoeuvre Navratilova. In the quarters at Forest Hills later that year, Martina ended Margaret's grand-slam singles career. Soon after, the Czech defected to the US and declared her sexual orientation.

In retirement, Margaret Court began to suffer "feelings of uselessness, inferiority, unworthiness". She found succour in Jesus, became a Pentecostal pastor and founded her own church in Perth. In 1990, she accused lesbians of ruining women's tennis and cited Navratilova as a bad example to young players.

A practising pescetarian, Navratilova eats nothing with fur or feathers. Although she played tennis right-handed, Margaret Court is a natural left-hander.

MORE THAN A CENTURY AFTER THE event, it remains unclear exactly why Chaja Rubinstein, 23, fled her native Poland and took lodgings with her uncle Louis Silberfeld, a shopkeeper in the hamlet of Coleraine, in the west of Victoria. Some say it was to escape an unwelcome suitor. Whatever her reasons, it turned out to be a smart move for the "haughty and difficult" daughter of a Cracow egg merchant.

She arrived in 1894, with no money and little English. Her stylish clothes and milky complexion did not pass unnoticed among the town's ladies, however, and she soon found enthusiastic buyers for the jars of beauty cream in her luggage. Spotting a market, she began to make her own. Fortunately, a key ingredient was readily to hand.

Coleraine might have been an "awful place" but it did not lack for lanolin. Sheep, some 75 million of them, were the wealth of the nation and the Western District's vast mobs of merinos produced the finest wool in the land, secreting abundant grease in the process. To disguise the sheep oil's pungent pong, Rubinstein experimented with pine bark, lavender and water lilies.

She also managed to fall out with her uncle. After a stint as a bush governess, she got a job as a waitress at the Winter Garden tearooms in Melbourne. There, she found an admirer willing to stump up the funds to launch her Crème Valaze, supposedly including herbs imported "from the Carpathian Mountains". Costing ten pence to make and selling for six shillings, it walked off the shelves as fast as she could pack it in pots. Now calling herself Helena, Rubinstein could soon afford to open a salon in fashionable Collins Street, selling glamour as a science to clients whose skin was "diagnosed" and a suitable treatment "prescribed".

Sydney was next, and within five years Australian operations were profitable enough to finance a Salon de Beauté Valaze in London. Then came Paris and New York.

Tiny in form, dictatorial in manner and famed for her parsimony, Madame Rubinstein roamed the globe, directing her ever-expanding empire and feuding with Elizabeth Arden. When her portrait was painted by William Dobell, she thought it "rather too much of a caricature", although that didn't stop her endowing a travelling scholarship for Australian artists.

Chaja Rubinstein never returned to Coleraine. She died in 1965, Princess Gourielli-Tchkonia, her business valued at $60 million. Her initial associates, the merinos, are believed to have all been eaten.

WHEN GENERAL SIR THOMAS BLAMEY heard that General Douglas MacArthur had been appointed supreme commander of Allied forces in the South-West Pacific Area, he was enjoying a drink in the first-class lounge of the Queen Mary, two days out of Cape Town. It was March 1942, a Japanese invasion appeared imminent, and Blamey was on his way home from the Middle East to take charge of Australia's military forces. MacArthur's appointment, he told his staff, was the best thing that could have happened.

A general's son who topped his class at West Point, MacArthur had led a combat division in France, risen to chief of staff of the US Army, and sent cavalry with sabres drawn against the wives and children of ragged veterans who'd marched on Washington demanding jobs. Recalled from retirement in 1941 to defend the Philippines, he escaped the island fortress of Corregidor by PT boat, flew to Australia and established his headquarters in Melbourne, 4000 kilometres from the front. It was at the Menzies Hotel on 29 March that he met Blamey for the first time.

The American supremo swept into the room as if preceded by a flourish of trumpets. Lean and clean-shaven, sporting his trademark corncob pipe, ostentatiously braided cap and Hollywood-style aviator sunglasses, he found himself face-to-face with a short, rotund figure wearing a grey moustache and Bombay Bloomers. At 57, seven years younger than MacArthur, Blamey was the very image of Colonel Blimp.

A drover's son who'd been promoted to full general only six months earlier, Blamey had a sharp mind for the strategic overview, fascistic tendencies and a reputation for favouritism, womanising and drunkenness. He'd never led troops in combat, and his most famous victories had been against the bolshie jobless during his tenure as Victoria's police commissioner.

If Blamey hoped for a rapport, he was soon disabused. Over the next three years, his staff officers were sidelined and the achievements of his troops deliberately downplayed. At Japan's formal surrender, MacArthur starred and Blamey was a mere extra, one of a shuffling queue of national representatives.

But magnanimity becomes the great, and in 1948 MacArthur invited him to Tokyo. Blamey fell asleep while visiting occupation troops. In 1950, Blamey received his field marshal's baton in hospital, and less than a year later he died of a cerebral haemorrhage. Meanwhile, MacArthur had been fired as UN commander in Korea for insubordination to his commander-in-chief, President Truman. He faded away in 1964. Blamey remains the only Australia-born field marshal.

AFTER MORE THAN 50 YEARS IN THE BUSIness, Jack Benny was nothing if not a trouper. When CBS dumped his long-running television show at the end of 1963, he pursed his lips, packed his violin and took his schtick on the road. In Australia, a consortium of promoters packaged him into a variety show that included acrobats, a popular chanteuse and, improbably, the country's paramount rocker, Johnny O'Keefe.

For all his tearaway image and microphone humping, JOK was no rock'n'roll rebel. He sold his music as an antidote to juvenile delinquency and banned long hair from his weekly television program *Sing, Sing, Sing*. And at 29, he was getting too old for the kid stuff. He yearned for the established mainstream stardom that a figure like Benny represented. With their shared billing in mind, he recorded the lush, syrupy ballad 'She Wears My Ring'.

The Sydney season opened on 7 March 1964. Benny, master of the pregnant pause, milked the laughs with his customary sophistication and O'Keefe belted out his trademark hits. Between them, they brought the house down.

Backstage, Benny was easy and unassuming, generous with his advice to the eager, vulnerable and moody O'Keefe. "Jack Benny was a marvellous influence on me. I would watch him every night. Up until that time, I'd not really emulated anybody but Little Richard."

The show got a tepid response in Melbourne, despite O'Keefe "working like a Trojan to win a response from the square dress circle", but the tour catapulted 'She Wears My Ring' straight into the charts.

No sooner had Benny returned home than the magic wore off. In May, *Sing, Sing, Sing* was relegated to an unwinnable slot, up against *Disneyland*. Then, in June, The Beatles arrived. By November, old-style rock was history and JOK was back in hospital with yet another of his nervous breakdowns. Within ten years, the St George Leagues Club was looking like a step up for the man once hailed as Australia's answer to Elvis.

Signing with NBC, Jack Benny returned to television. He retired after a season but continued to perform until his sudden death from pancreatic cancer in 1974. Johnny O'Keefe dwelt frequently on his memory, sometimes weeping in his dressing room for never having called to say how much he admired him. But there were tears aplenty by then, too many for even barbiturates to keep at bay.

UNTIL THE CAKES STARTED TO FLY, THE two artists were something of a mutual admiration society.

Thea Proctor was elegant, tasteful and generous, while Margaret Preston was flamboyant and stubbornly single-minded. One painted ladies on fans, the other preferred bottlebrush and banksia. But temperament and subject matter aside, they had much in common. Both were in their forties; each had spent many years abroad, soaking up techniques in the cultural capitals of Europe; both were well-known exponents of modernism, albeit in feminised forms.

Australia, Proctor declared, should be grateful to Preston for having rescued its wildflowers from the "rut of disgrace". Preston rendered Proctor's teapot in oils and showed her the mysteries of Japanese-style woodblock prints.

They first met in Sydney in the early '20s, recently returned expatriates fired with a desire to awaken Australia to the innovations they had encountered abroad. Instrumental in founding the Contemporary Group, they collaborated on articles and illustrations for *Home*, a decor magazine for the nation's more modish ladies. And although Proctor urged Australian artists to seek their place in the international modernist movement, whereas Preston advocated a national approach based on native vegetation and Aboriginal motifs, both were regarded as pushing the boundaries of Australian art.

The pairing reached its apogee in 1925, when the two held joint exhibitions in Melbourne and Sydney. Public reaction was gratifying but the big public galleries were slow to extend their recognition. If the starchy trustees of the Art Gallery of New South Wales were impressed enough to buy their work, it would be a victory for modernism and a feather in their individual chapeaux.

Proctor's studio shared the same George Street building as the Grosvenor Galleries, and they invited friends to join them there for tea after the opening. Margaret arrived bearing a box of cakes, asking immediately if the trustees had been and, if so, what they bought. Somewhat abashed, Thea was forced to admit that the grand arbiters had indeed decided to acquire a picture, and it was one of hers.

At this news, Margaret spat the dummy. She flung the cakes at Thea, turned on her heels, stormed out and disappeared "like Mephistopheles in a puff of smoke".

The careers of both artists continued to flourish, if not their friendship. In 1938, Proctor did not even mention Preston in an article on Sydney's outstanding modernist artists, except to say: "Mrs Preston's work is already widely known." To this day, postcards of Preston prints are consistent sellers in the gift shop of the Art Gallery of New South Wales.

Herr Hitler was busy in the Rhineland so Joseph Aloysius Lyons decided to pay a visit to Signor Mussolini instead. It was 1935 and collecting dictators was *de rigueur* for Australian politicians on visits to Europe.

'Honest Joe', then in his second term as prime minister, was returning home from imperial talks in London. A defector from Labor, he headed a conservative coalition. Popular, uncomplicated and widely admired, he was anti-conscription and anti-war. The slaughter of the Great War was a fresh memory and appeasement not yet a dirty word. From the war cemeteries of the Western Front, the 'tame Tasmanian' embarked for Italy.

Il Duce, poised to attack Abyssinia, believed that Britain's far-flung dominions bred "uncivilised *barbari*" beneath the intellectual level of Europeans. They offered, however, a useful side door into British imperial diplomacy. He greeted Lyons's arrival with an aeroplane escort and orchids for his wife, Enid. Impressed with fascism, while regarding it unsuitable for Anglo-Saxons, the Catholic couple headed first to the Vatican for an audience with the Pope, then to the Foreign Ministry, where Joe spent 20 minutes with Mussolini. To his amazement, the "genial" supremo spoke faultless English. He offered the Lyonses free passage to New York on an Italian liner. Relishers of official travel, they accepted. In New York, they sang his praises.

Two years later, Joe was back. This time, the meeting took place in Mussolini's grandiose office in the Palazzo Venezia. And this time, it was more than a mere courtesy call. The League of Nations was falling apart and general war was looming. Mussolini needed someone to champion the idea of an Anglo–Italian *détente* at upcoming talks in London, and Lyons was convinced that he was just the man to broker a breakthrough. Who better than a dominion statesman, a practitioner of consensus politics, to play go-between in European affairs?

Il Duce dominated the conversation. Lyons, often depicted in the Australian press as a plump and genial koala, was no match for his "massive intelligence" and the "completeness of his knowledge". His final words to Lyons were a message for Chamberlain: "Tell the British government I want peace."

Even as the armies of fascism were mobilising, Lyons continued to believe that his personal relationship with Mussolini might help avert the inevitable. Events proved otherwise. On 7 April 1939, Italy invaded Albania. The very same day, Lyons expired of a coronary occlusion, the first Australian PM to die in office.

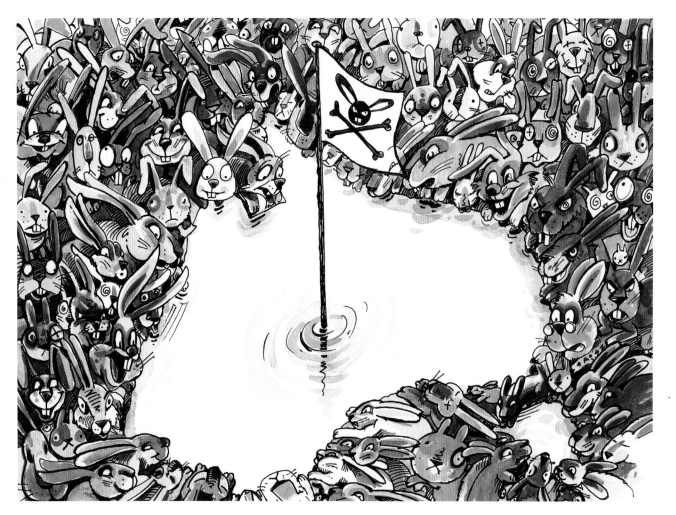

RABBITS ARE POOR CONSERVERS OF ENERGY. They can't adapt to drought. Their diet is not diverse. All in all, they are not well suited to the Australian environment. But when it comes to reproduction they can't be bettered. Mating takes 30 seconds, courtship included. In a single year, one doe can generate as many as 100 rapid-rooting offspring.

By 1950, the number of rabbits in Australia had reached 600 million. They devoured pastures and crops, ringbarked trees and spread erosion with their burrows. Shooting, poisoning, blasting, gassing, trapping, fencing, using ferrets or foxes and turning them into hats had all failed to make the slightest impact on their Malthusian multiplication.

Biological weapons were tested and failed. In 1888, Louis Pasteur sent a team from Paris armed with chicken cholera. It didn't work. Myxomatosis, a pox from South America, was proposed in 1919. The government rejected the idea on the grounds that it "wouldn't work".

Eventually, the CSIRO decided to give it a shot. In May 1950, a myxo-infected bunny was released at Gunbar in the Riverina. Through the winter, members of the wildlife research section tracked the progress of the virus. In August, they returned to Canberra "despondent, cold and wet". The disease worked in the warrens where it was introduced, but it didn't appear to spread.

Three weeks later, a case was reported in Corowa, more than 200 kilometres from Gunbar. By summer, it was in Queensland, spreading so fast the scientists couldn't keep up. The initial mortality rate was 99.5%. The smell of rotting flesh was everywhere in the bush. Within a year the rabbit population had dropped to 100 million.

The virus was spread by mosquitoes. So, too, was Murray Valley encephalitis, a virus potentially fatal to humans. It was a wet year, 1950, and there were a lot of mozzies. When people started dying, the CSIRO was blamed. To allay public concern, Australia's most prominent scientists, Prof. Macfarlane Burnet, Prof. Frank Fenner and Dr Ian Clunies Ross, had themselves injected with myxoma.

Within five years, the small number of resistant and immune rabbits had become a large number of resistant and immune rabbits. The 'accidental' release of calicivirus in 1995 again reduced Australia's rabbit population but the impact eventually began to wear off.

The Foundation for Rabbit-Free Australia promotes the Easter Bilby as an alternative to the Easter Bunny. Also known as the rabbit-eared bandicoot, the bilby is a marsupial omnivore known to eat baby rabbits. CSIRO scientists also invented Aerogard and Softly.

Sadly, only one of Australia's 114 official National Living Treasures has ever appeared in an episode of *Doctor Who*.

It happened in 1978 during the incarnation of the fourth Doctor, played by Tom Baker. Instantly identifiable from his curly hair, trademark long scarf, wide-brimmed hat, penchant for jelly babies and robotic dog called K-9, Baker appeared in 172 episodes over the seven years of his tenure of the role. But in only one of his TARDIS-propelled adventures did he share the small screen with Gai Smith, a young Australian actress who subsequently became Gai Waterhouse, racehorse trainer and ongoing ornament to the antipodean track.

"The Invasion of Time" begins with the Vardans, a shape-changing race of green-helmeted near-humans asking the Doctor to help them take over Gallifrey, home planet of the Time Lords. The Doctor agrees, but only as a ploy designed to outwit an invasion by the Sontarans, a bulbous-headed, green-blooded, three-fingered species of sinister, war-obsessed aliens.

Exiled to the Gallifreyan wastelands, the Doctor's female sidekick, Leela, is captured by a band of back-to-basics proto-ferals known as the Outsiders. One of these shaggy, pelt-wearing hunters is Presta, played by 23-year-old Gai. Togged out in headband and fur cape, Presta befriends Leela and a female Time Lord named Rodan, keeper of the transduction barrier. And when, in the final episode, Doctor Who re-enters the phone booth of destiny and departs, Presta is there to wave goodbye.

The only child of prominent Randwick trainer Tommy J Smith, Gai had already graduated from Sydney University, taken a walk around the modelling enclosure and appeared in an episode of *The Young Doctors*. Encouraged in her acting career by British actor James Mason, whose interest in racing had brought him into Tommy's ambit, she headed to London. But apart from a run in the BBC's premium sci-fi stakes, she failed to get out of the stalls.

Returning to Sydney, she became an apprentice at her father's Tulloch Lodge stables and married into the Waterhouse bookmaking dynasty. When husband Robbie was 'warned-off' as a result the 1984 Fine Cotton ring-in scandal, his spouse was included in the ban. Showing her mettle, she battled the Australian Jockey Club and won her trainer's licence in 1992. And when Tommy Smith became ill, he passed Tulloch Lodge on to her. Since then she has shaped some of Australia's finest horse flesh into champions.

Doctor Who is currently in his eleventh incarnation. Tom Baker became the voice of *Little Britain*. Despite the best efforts of the tenth Doctor, the Sontarans continue to pose a heavy-gravity threat.

FRANK ZAPPA WAS NO STRANGER TO AUStralia and its wildlife. Inspired by a monotreme encountered during his 1973 tour, the avant-rock polymath composed a complex jazz-fusion instrumental entitled 'Echidna's Arf (of You)'. Three years later, he came face-to-face with that even rarer antipodean creature, the little Aussie bleeder, Norman Gunston.

Gunston was then at the height of his fame as a no-holds-barred interviewer and multifaceted television variety-show host. His hugely successful program, *The Norman Gunston Show*, screened weekly on the ABC, and few visiting entertainers escaped being ambushed and subjected to a penetrating interrogation. During the dismissal of Whitlam, Gunston appeared on the steps of Parliament House, where he buttonholed political luminaries.

In January 1976, with a Mothers of Invention tour imminent, Gunston flew to Los Angeles for an on-camera chat with the notoriously abstruse Zappa. Instantly recognisable by his horseshoe moustache, pronounced proboscis and long hair, Zappa had progressed from Dada to doo-wop to big-band fusion, producing music simultaneously esoteric and seminal and collaborating with figures as diverse as Zubin Mehta and Keith Moon.

Initially the 35-year-old 'mother superior' was somewhat bemused by Gunston's digressive interview technique, but when the tissue-plastered Gunston produced a harmonica and suggested they jam together – "or you don't call it that over here, do you? You call it jelly" – Zappa promptly concurred. As he strummed a guitar, Gunston let rip with a blistering blues riff that deftly incorporated the *ABC News* theme.

"The boy has got a promising career," Gunston concluded of Zappa, urging Australians to give him a break on the upcoming tour. Zappa reciprocated by inviting Gunston to join the Mothers of Invention for the Sydney concert.

The gig took place at the Hordern Pavilion on 20 January. As the intro to 'The Torture Never Stops' kicked in, the little bleeder was called onto stage by the plaid-trousered Zappa, introduced as 'Blind Lemon' Gunston, and urged to blow.

Blow he did, on a mouth organ that "used to belong to Stevie Wonder". Two months later, he won a Gold Logie. Tapes of the concert remained in the vaults for more than a quarter of a century until their release as the album *FZ:OZ* in 2002. Shortly before his death in 1993, Zappa was appointed cultural attaché to his long-time fan Vaclav Havel, then president of Czechoslovakia. The Zappa Family Trust sponsors an echidna at the Los Angeles zoo.

Gunston went on to three more successful seasons before retiring. He has no children named Dweezil or Moon Unit but his progeny are legion.

Gough Whitlam & Zhou Enlai

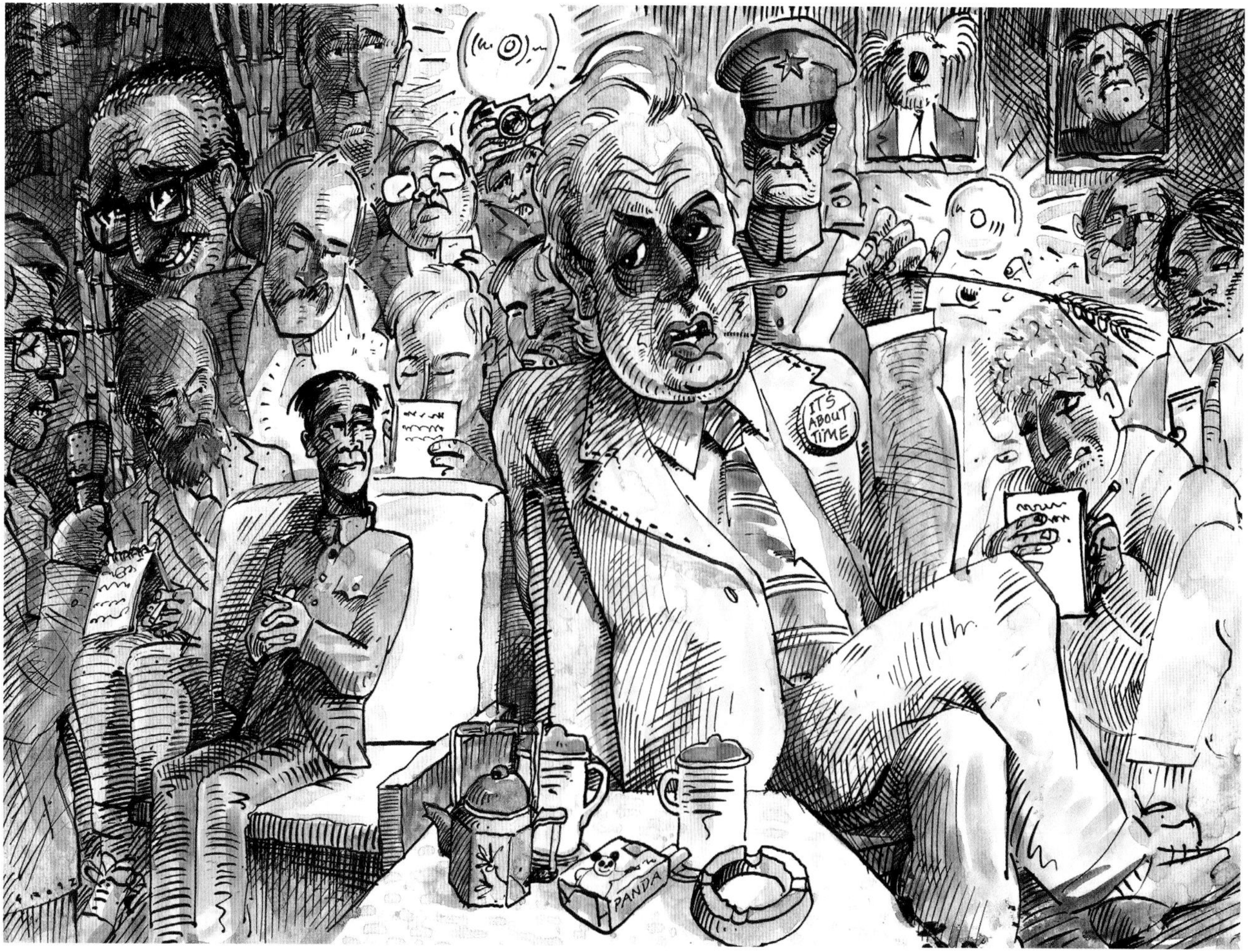

EARLY IN 1971, THE AUSTRALIAN WHEAT Board was worried that politics were getting in the way of business. To the Coalition government in Canberra, Red China was a downward-thrusting threat to be contained and isolated. To the AWB, it was a market at risk.

Enter Gough Whitlam, leader of an ALP that hadn't seen power for 20 years. Staking his electoral chances on his supreme self-assurance, he sent a message to the Chinese premier. Could they, he wondered, meet to discuss "matters of mutual concern"?

Zhou was a busy man. CEO of a nation mired in the chaos of the Cultural Revolution, he was hatching a scheme of world-changing audacity. *Come in July*, he cabled.

They met at midnight in the Great Hall of the People. To Whitlam's astonishment, the Australian press contingent was also invited. Teacups and tins of Panda cigarettes on low tables between them, the erudite Sydney barrister and the suave communist bureaucrat toured the international horizon, touching on the Vietnam War, wheat contracts and Canberra's recent statement that recognition of China was a long way off. Zhou's diplomatic experience was daunting, but the would-be Australian PM acquitted himself well.

As the meeting ended, Zhou dispensed with his interpreter. In perfect English, the elegant 73-year-old remarked on Whitlam's comparative youth. Whitlam replied that he was about to turn 55, the age at which Zhou represented China at the Geneva Conference. Zhou recalled the occasion. Dulles, the US secretary of state, had refused to shake his hand.

Two days later, in Shanghai, Zhou sent Whitlam a birthday cake. In the interim, Zhou had met secretly with Henry Kissinger, shaking hands on a deal that ended China's diplomatic and commercial isolation by the US. By the time Whitlam returned to Australia, the Labor leader's high-risk gamble seemed like an act of sublime prescience.

Eighteen months later he went back to China as Australia's prime minister. This time, there were bands and banquets and fulsome toasts. He was even presented to the emperor, the increasingly doddery Mao.

By then, Zhou had been diagnosed with bladder cancer, the Gang of Four was gunning for him and China seemed doomed to economic stagnation. He died in 1976, just a few months before the Great Helmsman. Whitlam, meanwhile, had succumbed to a different kind of death, relegated to the sidelines of history.

In March 1900 in Bloemfontein, in the Orange Free State, Andrew 'Banjo' Paterson attended a dinner hosted by the commander of the British forces occupying the town. The 36-year-old Sydney solicitor and poet was in South Africa to cover Australia's contribution to the stoush against the upstart Boers and he found himself seated beside the greatest literary celebrity of the Empire, the laureate of imperialism himself, Rudyard Kipling.

Kipling was not unaware of his dining companion's accomplishments. 'The Man from Snowy River' and 'Clancy of the Overflow' had made Paterson a national figure in Australia and the cantering cadences of his verse had much in common with Kipling's own galumphing style.

Paterson found Kipling "a little, squat-figured, sturdy man of about 40", a nervous, energetic gabbler with a tendency to Americanisms, a result of his long residence in Vermont. At first they talked books and newspapers, then politics. Kipling couldn't understand why there were so many radicals in Australia. Paterson "didn't feel equal to enlightening him". Kipling thought the Australians should stay on after the war to keep the Boers in line. Paterson didn't think the country worth fighting over – water was short and Cecil Rhodes had snaffled the best land.

A year later, Paterson called upon Kipling at his home in Sussex. Fancying himself a motoring correspondent, Kipling had just taken delivery of one of the newly invented machines, a Lanchester. Piling into the car, the two men hurtled about the South Downs like a scene from *The Wind in the Willows*, taking in views of the sea and raising a trail of leaves.

Pulling up outside a butcher's shop, Kipling pointed to a lamb carcass in the window and asked Paterson to guess its weight. Bush-born and raised, Paterson was only two pounds off the mark. Astonished, Kipling told the butcher to henceforth "buy all the Australian lamb you can get, and keep the money in the Empire". The butcher reckoned his customers were not much interested in the Empire, a sentiment seconded more politely by Paterson with the suggestion that Australians, likewise, "would always put Australia first".

Kipling's blustering certainties were cruelly punctured in 1915 when his son, John, was killed at the Battle of Loos six weeks after his eighteenth birthday. "If any question why we died," he later wrote, "tell them, because our fathers lied." The Banjo had signed up, too, although past 50. He drove an ambulance and looked after the horses. He died of a heart attack in 1941, and his ghost may be heard as you pass by the Northern Suburbs Memorial Gardens in North Ryde.

IN THE NORTHERN SUMMER OF 1932, Donald and Jessie Bradman spent their honeymoon crossing North America on a cricket tour sponsored by the Australian Dried Fruit Board. The Don's fame preceded him, the *New York Times* lauding the batsman as "the ring-tailed wallaby of the cricket crease".

It was a long and leisurely trip, and by the time the team reached California the Australians had seen the sights and played friendly games from Staten Island to Moose Jaw. In Burbank, in the last match of the tour, they met the Hollywood Cricket Club. Founded by *Prisoner of Zenda* star and former English Test captain Aubrey Smith, the HCC fielded a team that included such screen luminaries as Leslie Howard, Ronald Colman and Clive Brook, the original Phantom of the Opera. Its top-order batsman and wicketkeeper was Boris Karloff, who had shot to fame the previous year as the monster in *Frankenstein*, and was currently starring in *The Mummy* and shooting *The Mask of Fu Manchu*.

Despite his Slavic screen name, Karloff was very much an Englishman. Born in East Dulwich into a family of distinguished imperial administrators, William Pratt was educated in the manner befitting a chap of his breeding and era. He would, it was assumed, start a career in the mould of his father and brothers. But young Bill wanted to be an actor, and to spare his family's feelings he took his ambition abroad – first to Canada, where he changed his name, then to Los Angeles. For more than ten years he eked out a hardscrabble existence playing bit parts, and was into his forties by the time success arrived.

The Australians met the Hollywood team four times, punctuating the play with a whirl of social activity. None of the screen stars really shone on the field and it was a doddle for the Australians, who invariably won on the first innings. Karloff went in to bat after lunch on the first day, making seven of the HCC's 122 runs. On the second day, Bradman's twenty-fourth birthday, Karloff was bowled for 12. Two days later, The Don sailed for Australia and the Bodyline series.

The aloof, private batsman and the kindly one-man house of horror never met again. But in addition to a love of cricket, the two eventually had something else in common. In 1997 and 1998, each was commemorated on a special-issue postage stamp.

For more than six years, it hurtled through the stratosphere, a 77-tonne assemblage of micrometeoroid shielding, solar panels, coolant loops and booster rockets. But after 34,980 orbits of the Earth, Skylab was finally coming apart at the seams. The fuel tanks were almost empty and the gyroscope was cactus. The funds to haul it to a higher orbit hadn't materialised and a surge in solar activity was playing hell with the drag. There was only one place left for America's first space station to go.

Skylab – conceived by Wernher von Braun, commissioned by NASA and constructed by McDonnell Douglas – commenced its re-entry at 16.37 Coordinated Universal Time on 11 July 1979. Just after midnight local time, it burst through the cloud cover above Esperance, on the southern coast of Western Australia, shattering the calm with a series of sonic booms.

"We thought it was the end of the world," remembered Dorothy Andre, a local. Emergency services had turned out, just in case, and John Coates watched the show with the rest of the crew. "It was a terrific flame, like a burning plane, with all these little pieces shearing off. It was great."

It was also a financial windfall for a 17-year-old truck driver, Stan Thornton. When he learned that the *San Francisco Examiner* was offering a US$10,000 bounty for the first chunk of Skylab delivered to its office, he scooped a bagful of space junk off his roof and jumped on the first available flight. Arriving in the US with no passport and little more than a toothbrush and a few lumps of shrapnel, he pocketed the cash.

Dorothy Andre and her husband, Mervin, collected as much of the rest as they could find, including a Kombi-sized oxygen tank, and installed it in the Esperance Museum. Mervin, who was the shire president, also issued the US government with a ticket for littering.

Courtesy of the Kalgoorlie police, a sizeable piece of debris was transported to Perth, where it was displayed at the Miss Universe pageant, part of the WA sesquicentenary. During the coronation of Miss Venezuela, the platform collapsed under its weight. According to some sources, Miss Malta's right leg was fractured, Miss Brazil's gown was ripped and Miss Japan was treated for shock.

After Skylab, America's commitment to a permanent orbital station waned. But the drive for a human presence in space continues, and the collaborative International Space Station has been continuously inhabited since 2000 by a roster of astronauts from 14 countries. Three of them are up there right now, walking around.

Stan Thornton married his girlfriend and bought a house. As yet, the US hasn't paid the littering fine.

THE PRESIDENT OF THE UNITED STATES did not have a high opinion of the prime minister of Australia. "A pestiferous varmint", he called him. But William Morris Hughes didn't give a damn what Woodrow Wilson thought of him. He'd been called a lot worse, after all, and it hadn't done him any harm. The Labor Party had declared him a "rat" and expelled him from its ranks – yet here he was, two years later, still the PM and now backed by a whopping parliamentary majority. The British foreign secretary, Lord Robert Cecil, described him as "that shrimp" – yet he had secured an independent presence for Australia at the post-war negotiating table. President Clemenceau of France referred to him as a "cannibal" – but that was just good-natured Gallic humour.

It was 1919 and the world's statesmen were gathered in Paris to redraw the map of the world. Australia had expended much blood and treasure to win the peace, and Hughes was there to see that it got its fair share of the spoils. Wilson had grand schemes and high ideals but, when push came to shove, it would take more than a supercilious manner and some high-faluting cant to shut Billy Hughes up.

Wilson, a professor of jurisprudence and a former president of Princeton, had joined the war reluctantly and late. Not much interested in military affairs or the common soldier, he envisaged a peace based on decolonisation, disarmament and a League of Nations. Hughes, a former shearers' union organiser, had earned his law degree at 40, part-time. An eager warmonger, 'the little digger' wanted to hang the Kaiser, reduce Germany to penury and parcel out its overseas possessions to the victors.

The bone of contention was German New Guinea. Wilson wanted it declared a trustee territory of his proposed league. It was Australia's strategic front door, Hughes reckoned, and the size of our casualty list entitled us to outright ownership. "Am I to understand that Australia is prepared to defy the opinion of the whole civilised world, Mr Hughes?" Wilson brusquely demanded.

Hughes fiddled with his hearing aid and pretended not to have heard. Wilson, dripping sarcasm, repeated the question. "That's about the size of it, Mr President," drawled Hughes.

In due course, on a glorious June day, the plenipotentiaries assembled in the Hall of Mirrors to affix their signatures and seals to the Treaty of Versailles. Australia got New Guinea, and the civilised world got the League of Nations. Lacking a national seal, Hughes used the brass button from an Australian soldier's uniform.

WHEN DOUGLAS MAWSON TURNED UP AT Robert Falcon Scott's London office in January 1910, Scott assumed that the 27-year-old geology lecturer from Adelaide had come to enlist in his forthcoming expedition to the South Pole. Eight thousand men had already volunteered and Mawson was better qualified than any of them. He'd already explored large chunks of Antarctica, climbed its highest peak and reached Magnetic South.

Scott, by his own admission, had "no predilection for polar exploration". A naval commander in the peacetime doldrums, his burning desire was to "bring honour to the British Empire" and "defeat the foreigners" who were eyeing the prize. Mawson was "obviously capable and keen on his work", so Scott offered him a two-year contract, a salary and membership of the small sledging party that would make the final dash.

But Mawson wasn't looking for a job, and 90° South held no compelling attraction for him. There was no geographic value in a glory hunt and, although it had made him a popular hero, Scott's previous Antarctic foray had been a bit of a bungle. Mawson's interests were entirely scientific. He wanted Scott to drop him and a reconnaissance party on a section of uncharted coast to collect specimens, take measurements and undertake observations.

The two men talked for three hours and met again several times over the next fortnight. Mawson dined with Scott and his glamorous sculptor wife, Kathleen. But Scott couldn't spare the berths on his ship, so he turned Mawson down.

Undeterred, Mawson set about planning his own expedition. Waiting until Scott had sailed for Antarctica, he launched a funding campaign for the "Australasian Antarctic Expedition", its members drawn largely from Australian and New Zealand universities. In December 1911, he headed for the home of the blizzard. It was two years before he returned.

In that time, he established three bases, saw brave companions perish and hauled himself out of a crevasse, hand over frostbitten hand, during an epic month-long solo trek. The data he collected filled 22 volumes.

Scott, meanwhile, had done his dash. Big on pluck and short on luck, his party walked every step of the way, dragging their sledges and eating the pack ponies as they went. When he finally reached the Pole, Scott found he'd been beaten by one of those bally foreigners, the Norwegian Amundsen. On the way back, he perished, famously.

Mawson explored Antarctica again in 1929–31. He declared the continent 42% British, named part of it after the man who gave us Freddo Frog and died at home in ripe old age, esteemed by colleagues and country.

ALLEN GINSBERG SAW THE BEST MINDS OF his generation destroyed by madness, starving hysterical naked, dragging themselves through the negro streets at dawn looking for an angry fix. Then he went to the Northern Territory.

There, on a rainy evening in April 1972, the nudist, Buddhist, New York Jewish Beat poet came beard-to-beard with a man with 100 names, the ritual leader of the Rirratjingu clan of north-eastern Arnhem Land.

Ginsberg was bound for India, by way of the Adelaide Arts Festival. Since arriving in Australia, he'd been itching to hear Aboriginal music in its cultural context. Equipped with Tibetan finger cymbals and a pair of clapsticks, he flew to Nhulunbuy and headed south. The object of his journey was Wandjuk Marika, the famous song man, painter and cultural ambassador.

Reaching Yirrkala at dusk, the hipster bard found a funeral in progress. As his clan's mortuary man, Wandjuk was responsible for the correct conduct of the ceremony. He told the balding American – a man whose name meant nothing to him – that he was welcome to stay and observe. "Our funerals are as public as yours."

Ginsberg probably did not realise it, but he had stumbled upon one of the great expressions of Yolngu culture. Extending over a period of days, burial rites bring together a range of arts – coffin painting and body art, regalia of feathers and string, powerful dancing and sacred song cycles. Sitting quietly on the sidelines in the darkness, Ginsberg hummed along with the didgeridoo chorus.

The next morning, rain pelting down, Wandjuk and Ginsberg huddled in a hut on the beach near the site where the ancestral beings first landed on the mainland of Australia. Wandjuk had been singing all night. His voice was almost gone. He was exhausted. It was Ginsberg's turn.

Ginsberg chanted 'Hare Krishna' and tinkled his finger bells. He made no mention of *Kaddish*. To Wandjuk's amusement, he sang a song in Pitjantjatjara, which he had memorised. That afternoon, he returned to Darwin and departed for the Ganges. His subsequent published writings make no mention of Australia.

The following year, Wandjuk Marika helped establish the Aboriginal Arts Board. In 1984, he played a leading role in Werner Herzog's cinematic mishmash *Where the Green Ants Dream*, an experience that left him angry and disappointed. When he found his designs printed on tea towels, he stopped painting for ten years. He died in 1987, aged 60, of undetermined causes. Ginsberg died ten years later, burning, perhaps, for the ancient heavenly connection to the starry dynamo in the machinery of night.

THE KAIGUN RIKUSENTAI WERE HARD BAS-tards, elite marines from the naval ports of Kure and Sasebo who had bloodied their bayonets in China and the Philippines. Yet to be bested in battle, they finally met their match in the mud and rain of New Guinea.

In the early hours of 26 August 1942, a thousand of them landed on the northern shore of Milne Bay, under orders to capture and secure the airstrips. Confronting them were five battalions of Australian militia supported by a handful of RAAF Kittyhawks.

A malarial sinkhole cut by streams and soggy with sago and mangroves, Milne Bay had vital strategic significance. Port Moresby, the hinge on which Australia's defences hung, lay a scant 230 air miles away. A Japanese victory would outflank the fighting at Kokoda and seal its fate.

Caught on the hop, the defenders were initially pushed back. While reinforcements were hurried forward, Kittyhawks hammered the marines from tree-top level. The battle raged in a confusion of skirmishes and flanking movements fought in gusting rain and jungle mists. More marines landed, backed by naval gunfire. By the second night, they had reached No. 3 Airstrip, supported by two tanks and yelling phrases in English. Australian machine-gunners broke their impetus and the Japanese pulled back to regroup in the darkness.

The decisive engagement came at 3 a.m. on 31 August. As the Kaigun Rikusentai massed for attack among the palm trees beside the airstrip, flares lit their position. Artillery and mortars pounded them and a storm of rifle fire tore into their frontal charge. As wave upon wave rose to replace the fallen, they too were cut down. Just before dawn, "three bugle calls rang loud and clear", sounding the Japanese retreat.

Bitter fighting continued for another week, the marines setting lethal ambushes and murdering prisoners as they retreated towards their landing area. On 6 September, tails between their legs, they began to evacuate.

Over the next three years, units of the Kaigun Rikusentai fought do-or-die battles on dozens of Pacific islands. But the tide had turned. Japan had suffered its first defeat on land and the invincibility of the Japanese army had been shattered.

Despite delivering a victory, the Australian field commander, Major General Cyril Clowes, was belittled by his superiors, MacArthur and Blamey. Lacking friends in high places, he was sidelined for the rest of the war.

MORE THAN 30 YEARS AFTER HIS DISMISSAL from office, 'The Big Fella' was little more than a historical footnote, a near-forgotten figure. But to the 18-year-old Paul Keating, he was a living legend, a man still worth knowing.

A self-taught self-improver of the old school, Jack Lang worked his way up from a paperboy and horse-bus driver to lower-middle-class respectability as an auctioneer and real-estate agent. Elected premier of New South Wales in 1925, he introduced widows' pensions and workers' compensation, earning the undying enmity of the Establishment. Returning to power in 1930, he found himself neck-deep in a world financial crisis that had thrown 20% of the state's breadwinners out of work, a level comparable to Weimar Germany. His solution – a stimulus package funded by deferring interest payments to British banks – was slapped down by the federal Labor government. Facing confiscation of NSW's deposits at the Commonwealth Bank, he tried to run the state on a cash basis, providing the pretext for his sacking by the King's representative, a retired English air force officer.

A towering presence and a snarling, powerful orator with "more followers than friends", Lang remained a polarising presence in the ALP until he was finally expelled, in 1943.

Born the following year, Paul Keating was raised in a household where Lang's name cut no small ice. In 1962, a junior clerk at Sydney County Council and tyro apparatchik, young Paul visited the spartan Nithsdale Street office of the *Century*, Lang's one-man newspaper, and introduced himself to the ancient, near-deaf giant.

A creature of habit, Lang still wore a detachable collar and cuffs, a waistcoat with a gold watch chain and braces. Thrusting his massive jaw forward and banging on the table, "he talked at you".

Mr Keating, as Lang called him, was so impressed that he came back. Twice a week for the next eight years, he helped the old warhorse with the proofs of his paper and soaked up Labor lore, tales of treason and loyalty larded with Lang's take-no-prisoners philosophy.

A quick study, the disciple was soon throwing his own political punches. At 25, he was a federal MP. In 1971, as the member for Blaxland, he finally succeeded in having Lang, then 95, re-admitted to the Labor Party.

Lang died in 1975, shortly before another dismissal swept Keating out of his first ministry.

IN THE LEAD-UP TO A FEDERAL ELECTION, THE Labor Opposition leader is shot at point-blank range as he leaves a rowdy public meeting. The bullet, fired from a sawn-off rifle, shatters the window of his car, spattering him with broken glass and bullet fragments. His would-be assassin drops the gun and runs away. He is chased, caught and overpowered without further incident. A 19-year-old factory hand, he says he wants to be remembered by history for killing somebody important. He chose his target "because I don't like his politics".

The Opposition leader, in shock and bleeding from the face, has narrowly escaped death. Deflected on impact with the window, the bullet has lodged in the lapel of his coat. The gunman is declared criminally insane, sentenced to life imprisonment and incarcerated in a psychiatric prison. His victim sends him a letter of forgiveness and returns to the election campaign, in which national security is a major issue. When Labor is thrashed at the polls, he is compelled to cede the leadership to his younger, charismatic deputy.

His successor eventually steers Labor to victory and the former leader retires from parliament. Three years later, the gunman is set free and given a Literature Board grant to write poetry.

The year was 1966 and Arthur Calwell had been the Labor leader for six years. As the post-war immigration minister, he'd opened the country to huge numbers of refugees and new settlers, albeit on a racial basis. He was a deeply principled man but his pugnacious, old-fashioned style was unsuited to the age of television. His outspoken opposition to American bases, conscription and the war on Vietnam made him unpopular, and Whitlam's supporters viewed him as an electoral liability.

Peter Kocan was a casebook disturbed loner. Fatherless, disadvantaged and victimised, he left school at 14 and drifted though a series of menial jobs. On 21 June, he entered the Mosman Town Hall with a .22 hidden under his overcoat, mingled with the crowd and approached Calwell just as he was being driven away. Assuming the man was a well-wisher, Calwell began to wind down his window. Kocan aimed at his jugular and pulled the trigger.

In the asylum, a fellow inmate introduced him to the works of Rupert Brooke. He began to study literature, philosophy and history, and to write poetry. Two of his collections were published while he was still locked up, and his subsequent work draws on his experience of psychosis and imprisonment. His novella *The Cure* won the 1983 NSW Premier's Literary Award for fiction. In his science-fiction novel *Flies of a Summer*, he portrays a future in which all memories of the past have been erased.

Arthur Calwell, who died in 1973, is often remembered for saying "Two Wongs don't make a white." He was misquoted.

When the Grecian songbird Nana Mouskouri embarked on her first Australian tour in 1976, she was greeted with rave reviews and the adulation of fans. Among the raven-haired nightingale's keenest admirers was a communist writer almost 20 years her senior.

Frank Hardy had been a public figure for decades. His roman à clef *Power Without Glory* had created a publishing and legal sensation and become the must-see television series of the year. *But the Dead Are Many* had won him international plaudits, and his yarns about finagling dustmen and mug punters had carved him a niche as the oracle of the lumpen proletariat.

Despite his notoriety and success, Hardy was not a happy man. Socialist realism, lefty navel-gazing and shaggy-dog stories cut no ice with the Australian literati. Money ran through his fingers. The comrades were jack of him, his marriage was over and his lovers had deserted him. Pushing 60, he needed a new muse.

Nana Mouskouri's wistful stage presence, easy-listening vocals and geeky glasses had made her one of the biggest-selling acts in the world. She'd never heard of Frank Hardy.

When the tour reached Sydney, he arranged a backstage introduction, then deluged her with phone calls. Eventually she suggested they meet in Paris, her home since the early '60s. Hardy "snatched at the idea, like a prisoner who suddenly thinks of a plan to escape".

Their rendezvous took place at the Café de Flore, that most famous of intellectual hangouts. By then, Nana had boned up on Hardy's books and they'd talked at length on the phone. She was 41, recently divorced, the mother of two young children and "so anxious that my throat was dry".

Hardy was "agitated, a little out of breath, constantly fiddling". They talked matters of the heart. For all the novelist's "indefinable attraction", though, Nana didn't like being rushed. But, yes, she would see him again. He moved to the south of France, breathed deep the artistic atmosphere and accompanied Mouskouri on her European tours. She gave him *The Little Prince*. He called her 'Pilgrim' and knocked out a novel in 23 days beneath her face on a garlanded poster. But when he declared his love, she demurred, opting instead for her business manager.

The *grande affaire* spent, Frank Hardy returned home. He died in 1994, obstreperous as ever. That year, Nana Mouskouri was elected to the European parliament on a right-wing ticket. After 450 albums in 15 languages, she's still wearing the glasses.

ON THE EVENING OF 10 FEBRUARY 1964, the aircraft carrier HMAS *Melbourne*, flagship of the Royal Australian Navy, and the Daring-class destroyer HMAS *Voyager* were conducting a night exercise to the south-east of Jervis Bay. Two Sea Venom fighters from the naval air base at Nowra were attempting a 'touch and go' landing on the carrier's flight deck. As 'plane guard', the *Voyager*'s job was to escort the *Melbourne* at a distance of 1500 yards, ready to recover any aircraft that ditched into the drink.

The sea was smooth with a low swell, the night was dark with no moon or clouds, and both ships were lit only with operational lights. As the *Melbourne* changed course, the *Voyager* was signalled to make corresponding adjustments to its position. Normally this would mean allowing the *Melbourne* to pass ahead, then crossing its stern before taking up station on its starboard quarter.

As the 20,000-ton carrier completed its manoeuvre, the *Voyager* suddenly turned back across its bows. Despite desperate attempts to avert a collision, the carrier struck the destroyer amidships, slicing it in half. The *Voyager*'s captain and bridge officers were killed by the impact. Destabilised by the weight of its gun turrets, the ship's bow section capsized, then sank.

For the next three hours, the crew of the badly damaged *Melbourne* worked feverishly to rescue battered and bleeding survivors from the water and the aft of the *Voyager*, which remained defiantly afloat. Apart from other injuries, most had swallowed sea water and fuel oil. In all, 82 officers and sailors lost their lives. Shortly after midnight, Captain Robertson, the recently appointed commander of HMAS *Melbourne*, signalled fleet headquarters: "*Voyager* has sunk."

Two royal commissions failed to adequately account for the accident. Allegations were made that the *Voyager*'s captain was an alcoholic and an amphetamine user. Poor visibility, a mix-up over signals and a navigation 'fishtail' were variously blamed. Lies were told and officers covered each other's backs. Surviving seamen battled for decades for compensation.

After repairs, the *Melbourne* resumed duty. In June 1969, during SEATO exercises in the South China Sea, it collided with the destroyer USS *Frank E Evans* in almost identical circumstances to the *Voyager* disaster. Seventy-four American sailors died. The *Melbourne* was exonerated. After decommissioning in 1982, it was bought by a Chinese scrap-metal company and broken up.

The wreck of the *Voyager* lies in 600 fathoms of water, 20 nautical miles east of the Point Perpendicular lighthouse. The current HMAS *Melbourne* is a guided-missile frigate, and the lead ship for the Nulka expendable-decoy system. According to the Navy, 'nulka' is an Aboriginal word meaning 'be quick'.

If Nellie Melba and Enrico Caruso were each major attractions, their double act was a sensation. Between them, the imperious Australian soprano and the effusive Italian tenor transformed *La bohème* from a slow-burn sleeper into a blockbuster hit that is still putting bums on seats a century later. Theirs was the golden age of the warbler, a time when new technologies were turning opera singers into household names and bel canto into big bucks. Melba knew exactly what she was worth and she made it her business to collect every plaudit and every penny of it. Woe betide anyone who tried to short-change, outshine or upstage her.

Nor was Caruso any slouch in the fame-and-fortune department. His velvet voice won him millions of fans, and his name on a phonograph record or a playbill was a licence to print money. But the puckish poor boy from backstreet Naples was generous to a fault and wore his celebrity a lot more lightly than the tightwad-prima donna from Presbyterian Ladies College in Melbourne.

If Melba was the queen of the opera, London's Covent Garden was her palace, one she guarded jealously from new and rival talent. Little wonder the up-and-coming Caruso could not stop himself from committing a diva-deflating act of lèse-majesté. During the 1902 season of *La bohème*, while singing the tender aria 'Che gelida manina, se la lasci riscaldar' (*Your tiny hand is frozen, let me warm it here in mine*), he covertly pressed a hot Italian sausage into her captive hand. As the starvation-dazed seamstress Mimi, she should probably have snaffled it. Instead she gave a yelp and sent it skittering across the stage, to the puzzlement of the audience.

"You filthy dago," she hissed.

"English lady no like sausage?" he asked, feigning hurt. Dry toast was more to Melba's taste, of course, and a poached peach with ice-cream and raspberry sauce, although she did complain that she was being chiselled out of her royalties by Ritz and Escoffier. Caruso, when he wasn't slipping the sausage to sopranos, enjoyed nothing more than a hearty feed of spaghetti with mushrooms and chicken livers, a dish that came to bear his name. His career was cut short at 48 when he succumbed to a fatal attack of pleurisy, a disease of the lungs.

Acutely image-conscious to the last, Melba died at 69 of septicemia resulting from a facelift. The face survived. It can be seen on the $100 note, a fact that would surely have pleased the original Material Girl.

In February 1904, Stella Miles Franklin – then aged 24 – received an admiring letter from a 60-year-old former bullock-driver named Joseph Furphy. He requested a photograph and proposed that they meet.

My Brilliant Career, Franklin's semi-autobiographical novel about a spirited teenager's rebellion against stultifying convention, had appeared three years earlier. It was the only Australian novel published in the year of Federation. Described with pride by Henry Lawson in the preface as "just a little bush girl", Franklin was being hailed by the leading literary lights of the day as a significant voice in national letters.

Furphy, too, was an author. A kind-hearted, self-educated bush philosopher, he'd spent the previous 15 years working at his brother's foundry in Shepparton, where he wrote at night in a corrugated-iron shed out the back. The result was a sprawling, discursive manuscript of 1200 handwritten pages, sent on spec to the editor of the *Bulletin* with the description "temper, democratic; bias, offensively Australian". Whittled to a digestible size, *Such Is Life* was published under the nom de plume Tom Collins.

The pair met at Easter, in the vestibule of the Melbourne GPO. From there, they drifted to the art gallery, trailed by female fans who'd gotten wind of Franklin's presence.

Seated in a small circle before Longstaff's *The Sirens*, they didn't have much chance for conversation, what with Franklin's "merry laugh" resounding through the gallery and the swarming attention of her admirers. The shy, courteous old bullocky later joked that he had feared arrest as the responsible male, the "solitary he-feller of the synod". After the gallery, he took Franklin to Cole's Book Arcade, where he gave her a "certain publication" which modesty forbore him naming.

It was their sole meeting. Joseph Furphy went home to Shepparton and later moved to Perth to live with his sons. He died there in 1912.

Miles Franklin, daunted by the literary expectations laid upon her and the reaction of family members to their depiction in her novel, went to Chicago to work for a women's trade-union organisation. She lived abroad until 1932.

In 1944, she wrote a biography of Furphy – our "bush Hamlet" – in painful collaboration with Kate Baker, who was one of the posse that tailed her to the art gallery. "*Such Is Life*," she wrote, "is more than a novel … it is our *Don Quixote*, our *Moby-Dick*."

Her bequest, the eponymous literary prize, was first awarded to Patrick White. In 1995, the judges gave it to a Ukrainian-impersonating plagiarist. *Such Is Life* remains a classic which nobody reads and even fewer comprehend.

Lionel Rose was nearing the end of a hard training session when he got the message that Elvis Presley wanted to meet him. It was December 1968 and the 20-year-old Aboriginal boxer had come to Los Angeles to defend his world bantamweight title against Mexican challenger Chucho Castillo. But the bout was still two days away, and an invitation from the King was not something to be passed up. Elvis was, after all, a big favourite of Lionel's mum. Rose "pulled off the gloves, jumped under the shower and drove straight to the MGM lot".

Presley was shooting a movie, probably *The Trouble With Girls*, one of the string of mediocre musicals that occupied his time and talents in the hiatus between his hip-grinding glory days and his decline into a Las Vegas grotesque. A runner on the set, a fight fan, had suggested the get-together, judging that the two men would get along well. He was right. They spent two hours together, talking about music and the manly arts.

Rose had grown up in poverty near Drouin in Gippsland, learning to box from his father, a fighter in tent shows. While still in his teens, the shy boy from the bush defeated Japan's seemingly invincible Fighting Harada to become the champion of the world and a hero to Aboriginal Australia.

Elvis, a ready scrapper since his early days on the road, had picked up a strong interest in karate during his stint in the army. A certified black belt, he did his own fight sequences in his movies, including *Kid Galahad*, in which he played a boxer. At 33, he was still fit and trim. "Not fat and flabby like later," Rose recalled.

As well as conversation, there was a little light sparring – strictly for the camera – and an autographed US dollar bill as a gift for Lionel's mum back home. Would Elvis ever come to Australia? Rose wondered. Too far away, said the King. They parted as friends, the young boxer "pleased as punch" by the encounter.

Rose returned to his training and beat Castillo on points, eventually notching up 53 professional wins before retiring in 1976. Between bouts, he displayed a softer side as a crooner of country ballads. 'I Thank You' and 'Pick Me Up on Your Way Down' both topped the charts. There were rough patches, but he never lost the affection of the public. Elvis, meanwhile, kept getting bigger. And bigger. And bigger. In 1977, he was felled by a lethal sucker punch from a fried peanut-butter and banana sandwich.

THE COMBINATION WAS UNTRIED BUT promising. To a well-pickled English favourite add a hearty Australian staple. Mix together in a selection of French cookware, season with mutual respect, sit with a glass of wine and let the flavours mingle.

Elizabeth David was the closest thing to culinary royalty that Britain had ever produced. Her *Mediterranean Cooking* and *French Country Cookbook* were credited with introducing the courgette to a rationed and ravenous population and shining a garlic-infused blaze of southern sunlight into the cabbage-reeking corners of the post-war English kitchen. No matter that most of her compatriots stuck with their cod-and-chips, Elizabeth David had brought an aura of peasant chic to a job for which middle-class women could no longer find the servants.

Notoriously crabby, David shunned publicity, preferring to let her books speak for themselves. In 1965 she put writing on the backburner to open a cookware shop in London's fashionable Belgravia.

In 1970, Margaret Fulton paid her a visit. Ten years younger, Fulton was a household name in Australia. Beginning her gastronomic career at 18 as a gas-company oven demonstrator, she'd qualified in vegetable chopping at East Sydney Tech, sold pressure cookers and Rice Bubbles, and eventually garnered a vast readership through the pages of *Woman's Day*. For the housewives of a burgeoning and affluent suburbia, she made food a means of self-expression and a road to adventure. She also made her recipes foolproof, partly by the simple but radical innovation of listing all the required ingredients first. *The Margaret Fulton Cookbook*, published in 1968, sold more than a million copies.

Fulton had read that David radiated an inner elegance. "I thought it was a load of tripe," she recalled. But she was immediately won over. David "had soup stains down her very English twin-set and her teeth were stained from drinking red wine" but her face "declared her passion for living life to the full".

David knew of Fulton and acknowledged her as part of a shared tradition. They retired to the backroom and ate lunch with the staff, each equally sure of herself. Margaret was thinking of opening a shop. Did Elizabeth have any advice? Be true to yourself, she suggested. Stock only things you'd use yourself.

Fulton decided to stick to recipe books. Three years later, an acrimonious David severed ties with her cookware shop.

Despite their best intentions the two never met again. Elizabeth David died in 1992. In 2004, Margaret Fulton celebrated her eightieth birthday, campaigned with Greenpeace against GM food, and published a revised and updated version of her eponymous classic.

EVERYBODY WANTED TO BE NICOLAE Ceausescu's friend – the United States, Britain, China and the premier of Western Australia. To the Americans and the Chinese, the infamous Romanian dictator was a geopolitical thorn in the side of the Soviet Union. To Brian Burke, he was a business bonanza waiting to happen. And so, in July 1987, the Don of the Swan set out to woo the Danube of Thought.

Already a major customer for Australian coal, Romania was a potential gateway to Eastern Europe for Pilbara iron ore. Aware of Ceausescu's aversion to foreign debt, Lang Hancock had devised an elaborate deal to swap raw minerals for railway wagons. A delegation of politicians, public servants, businesspeople and union officials was assembled. Burke's job was to front the pitch.

The Genius of the Carpathians was somewhere in the port city of Constanta. After a guided tour of the newly completed Danube–Black Sea canal, the Westralians set off for their meeting with the megalomaniac so vicious that even other communist despots detested him. Shunted from palace to palace through austere streets heavy with paranoia, Burke and his entourage were eventually ushered into Ceausescu's presence.

The tyrant sat across the conference table, backed by stony-faced Securitate bodyguards and flanked by functionaries. Burke laid out the proposition. Ceausescu grunted. An underling translated. Il Conducator, he said, could make anything possible. Ceausescu grunted again.

The delegation returned home with no immediate results to show for its efforts, apart from a sightseeing trip to Dracula's castle and the dose of gastro which swept through its ranks in the days following the meeting.

When Ceausescu visited Perth the following year, he was put up in Government House. But by then, the wheels were falling off the WA Inc. wagon. Collusion between Burke's inner circle and certain prominent businessmen was revealed to have rorted the state of $600 million, and Burke had quit the premiership to become the ambassador to Ireland and the Holy See. Soon after, he was charged with fraud and deception, and convicted of stealing campaign funds – money he'd spent on his stamp collection. The Hancock plan never got off the ground.

But all's well that ends well. Nicolae Ceausescu was executed by his own henchmen. Brian Burke continues to exert considerable influence in WA Labor and business circles. And Australia's relations with Romania turned out to be a licence to print money. The country's banknotes are today manufactured in Craigieburn, Victoria.

I WENT TO PATAGONIA AND ALL I GOT WAS THIS CRAPPY MUG

It was 1980 and Robyn Davidson was 30, unknown and working on the manuscript of her first book. London was cold and wet and a long way from her subject matter, but she'd found congenial digs in Doris Lessing's self-contained flat and exile companionship in two cockatiels she'd ransomed from a street market. The birds were flapping around the flat, pining for far horizons, when Bruce Chatwin knocked on the door.

The celebrated author of *In Patagonia* had heard about Davidson and her dromedary-propelled outback odyssey, and decided he should meet her. Chatwin was a decade older, "a very beautiful-looking man, I assumed gay, very witty with a questing intellect".

They passed the afternoon in congenial chat. About nomads, mainly. Chatwin wanted to know all about Aborigines, but when Davidson got around to land rights, his curiosity took a dive. Politics bored him and the conversation moved to gossip about notable figures he'd encountered. "He was a marvellous mimic," Davidson recalled. By the afternoon's end, Chatwin had done a ripper impersonation of Indira Gandhi and acquired a list of useful contacts in Alice Springs.

Two years later, Davidson was back in Australia. Her book, *Tracks*, had catapulted her to unsolicited celebrity as the 'Camel Lady', and she was doing the famous-author thing at Adelaide Writers' Week. Also on the bill was Bruce Chatwin. He arrived with a friend, Salman Rushdie, and the two chaps promptly lit out for the Territory to climb Uluru and commune with the natives.

Later, while Chatwin was inflating his outback observations into *The Songlines*, Davidson visited him in Oxford to confer and advise. By that stage, she and Rushdie were a number, their affair the talk of book town. By the time *The Songlines* appeared and *The Satanic Verses* sent the mad mullahs reaching for their scimitars, Davidson's restless feet had carried her to far Rajasthan, where she found other camels and other nomads and a new book, *Desert Places*.

Bruce Chatwin died in Nice in 1989, taken by AIDS at 49. After half a lifetime of waking up beside hairy beasts, Davidson has returned to live permanently in Australia. Coming home, she calls it. Of the two cockatiels, nothing further is known. Flighty creatures, they have left no tracks.

IN THE DYING DAYS OF THE WAR TO END ALL wars, Anzac horsemen cantered down the Golan Heights and put the Ottoman army to flight. Damascus lay before them, theirs for the taking. On the night of 30 September 1918, they took it.

Early the next morning, their commander arrived. The son of a New South Wales grazier, Harry Chauvel was a born cavalry officer. He was 53, the first Australian to command a corps, and Damascus was the pinnacle of his career as a field soldier.

Chauvel found his local liaison officer, a 30-year-old Oxford archaeologist named TE Lawrence, outside Government House, "attired as the sherif of Mecca" and surrounded by a crowd of exuberant Arabs.

Lawrence had spent the previous two years raising a revolt in the desert, an enterprise he described as a "sideshow of a sideshow". Emaciated, exhausted and agitated, he informed Chauvel that a new civil administration had been formed and suggested the Australian troops be kept outside the city, well away from its discipline-sapping temptations.

Immersed in the logistics of men and mounts, prisoners and provisions, Chauvel took this advice at face value. But Colonel Lawrence had divided loyalties. He'd promised Damascus to the Hashemite king, Faisal bin Hussein. The Arab army was running late and its triumphal entry into the ancient capital would fall flat unless Lawrence could buy it some time.

By afternoon, the jubilation of the liberated Damascenes turned to pillage and revenge, and Chauvel realised that his subordinate was trying to put one over him. Faisal's supporters were clearly incapable of maintaining order, so Chauvel paraded the Light Horse through the streets. Their emu feathers had an immediate calming effect on the population.

When Faisal eventually galloped into town, he was met with bad news. Syria and Lebanon were promised to France, and the British were keeping Palestine. Chauvel was the minute-taker at the meeting. Lawrence denied knowledge of the sell-out and asked to go home.

After the war, Lawrence lobbied for the Arab cause, denigrated Chauvel in his empurpled and unreliable memoir, *The Seven Pillars of Wisdom*, joined the RAF under a false name, died in a motorcycle crash in 1935, and was later played on the screen by a much taller actor. Harry Chauvel became chief of staff, trained a generation of Australian officers and died in harness at the age of 80. Inspired by his memory, his nephew Charles made *Forty Thousand Horsemen*, a film in which Peter O'Toole does not appear. In 1921, the British installed Faisal as the king of Iraq.

ONE LUNCHTIME IN AUGUST 1948, PETER Finch was doing Molière on the shop floor at O'Brien's glass factory in Sydney when Laurence Olivier and Vivien Leigh turned up.

Olivier and Leigh were the king and queen of the British theatre. He had been knighted for conspicuous enunciation in tights and she had won an Academy Award for her Scarlett O'Hara. Married since 1940, the golden couple were touring Australia to stiffen the post-war cultural sinews of the Commonwealth and raise money for the cash-strapped Old Vic theatre company.

With his expressive cheekbones, resonant voice and luxuriant wavy hair, Finch was Australia's most promising actor. A veteran of outback tent shows, a *Dad and Dave* film, army service in the Middle East and a role in *The Rats of Tobruk*, he wowed the factory workers and sandwich-munching secretaries. Vivien and Larry thought him marvellous. If ever he was in England, he should get in touch.

Three months later, Finch arrived in London and Olivier put him on contract. By then, all was not well with the royal marriage. On their return from Australia, Vivien announced that she now loved her husband "sort of, well, like a brother".

Soon after, while playing Blanche DuBois, her manic-depression became a full-blown pathology. She slept with everyone and anyone, suffered delusions and started to go completely starkers. By the time she won an Oscar for *Streetcar*, she was beyond even Hollywood's pale. To get her out of sight, she was offered the lead in *Elephant Walk*, to be shot in Ceylon. Her male co-star would be Peter Finch.

There had been earlier rumours of an affair but things came to a head during the filming. Both were drinking heavily and they spent the nights together on a hillside under the stars. The script called for Leigh to escape a giant anaconda and a herd of stampeding elephants. It was too, too much. She slipped into paranoia, began to hallucinate and trailed after Finch, calling him Larry.

Olivier was summoned, "anxious to see the state of the union". He abdicated his wife to his protégé and returned home "in a soft coat of numbness".

The shoot was cancelled and Leigh replaced with Elizabeth Taylor. The lovers ran off to the south of France, held hands at Stratford and drove poor Larry to his wit's end. Vivien was, after all, Lady Olivier.

It was all too fraught for Peter, too. He went on to *A Town Called Alice* and, ultimately, his own Oscar, posthumously, in 1977, a category first. By then, the curtain had long fallen on the fragile beauty that had been Vivien Leigh.

THE MEETING HAD BEEN IN PROGRESS FOR five hours when Conrad Black strode into Kerry Packer's sumptuous suite at the Savoy.

It was June 1991 and Packer was in England to play polo. Between chukkas, he was assembling a consortium to bid for the John Fairfax company, which was in receivership. Black, the flamboyant Canadian media tycoon, wanted a piece of the action. So, too, did Malcolm Turnbull, lawyer turned investment banker.

Packer needed partners to get around Australia's media ownership laws; Black had global ambitions and a bulging war chest; and Turnbull had dealt himself a hand at the big boys' table as the champion of Fairfax's principal creditors, US bondholders, whose litigation could tie up any takeover indefinitely. A snug syndicate would be in everybody's interest.

Black found Turnbull, ten years his junior, to be affable, well scrubbed and persuasively articulate, despite having "considerable difficulty maintaining his self-control against an onslaught of unimaginable compulsive inner tensions and ineluctable ambitions". He quickly assessed Turnbull's nuisance value, rating it high.

Numbers were crunched, jobs allocated and Tourang was up and running. Packer went back to his ponies and Black returned to Canada for the summer.

In the months that followed, the fight for Fairfax became Australia's premier three-ring circus. Alternative bidders came and went; journalists railed; Malcolm Fraser and Gough Whitlam joined hands to lead the fight against greater media concentration.

But behind the scenes, the Tourang coalition was fraying. Black's lieutenants thought Turnbull wore too many hats. Turnbull, a protégé of Packer, was keen to signal his independence. The knives were out.

"I explained to Black that if you want to be an assassin, you have to be prepared to have a little blood on your hands," Turnbull recalled. But when the blow came, he blamed Packer: "I was turfed because Kerry Packer knew I was my own man."

Minus Malcolm, then Kerry, Conrad won the bid. At the first AGM, he accused Turnbull of gouging $6.3 million out of the deal "for minimal services". Four years later, he sold up and shot through.

He is now Baron Black of Crossharbour, his Canadian citizenship ditched for a seat in the House of Lords, and is facing US warrants for racketeering, money laundering and fraud. The FBI raided his New York apartment. Sotheby's is suing him.

Turnbull's fortunes are flourishing, despite the setback of the republic referendum. Richly rich, a Liberal MP, he has pitched himself as a future prime minister. Even the old sores have healed. At Kerry Packer's funeral, he led the crowd singalong of 'C'mon Aussie, C'mon'.

W HEN HER FRIEND CONNIE POINTED OUT the advertisement in the morning paper, Rose Lacson told her she was crazy. She was just passing through, after all, on a 30-day tourist visa. A prolonged stay in Perth was not something she'd considered.

There was also the little matter of experience. Admittedly, Rose had been around the block more times than average for a convent-educated daughter of the Manila middle class. She'd already been an interior decorator, an insurance broker, a black-marketeer and a pantyhose model. She'd even tried her hand at matrimony a couple of times, but the self-assured 32-year-old had never before been a housekeeper. A servant, no less. Hired help.

Still, it was worth considering. She was at something of a loose end. Business prospects were unpromising, her daughter's boarding-school fees needed to be paid, and Connie was eager for the companionship of a fellow Filipina. Rose dialled the number and, crazy or not, found herself with the job.

Her first day, 21 April 1983, was "a fiasco". Her employer had already left for work. Although he was well-off, his Dalkeith house reflected a tight fist. The washing machine was dilapidated and the vacuum cleaner was antique. Come noon, he stomped through the front door for his customary lunch of cold meat with bread and butter, eaten alone in the television room. More than twice Rose's age, he was gruff and abrupt.

"Good afternoon, sir," said Rose. "I am here to serve you."

Langley George Hancock was newly widowed. Hope, his wife of 37 years, was less than three weeks dead. His daughter, Gina, was not a naturally warm person. The emperor of the Pilbara had nobody to care for him. The cantankerous old 'knockabout bushman' was lonely.

He took a long, lingering look at the new maid, peering through thick glasses at her denim mini and thin white blouse. "Hello, hello, hello!" he said.

Before long, Rose was finding ways to make the boss feel special – like turning down the collar of his tennis shirt or giving him a stress-relieving massage. The skinflint prospector had met his match. Two years later, Rose Lacson became Rose Hancock in a poolside ceremony at the Sydney mansion of Lang's millionaire tax advisor. For a wedding gift, he ordered the construction of Prix d'Amour, a home truly worthy of his bride.

It was there, in the guesthouse, that Lang died in 1992. Nagged to death, according to Gina. Soon after, Rose married a real-estate developer. Prix d'Amour has since been bulldozed and the site subdivided.

S IR EUGENE GOOSSENS WAS A MAN WHO liked a little magic in his life. Sex magic, to be specific.

Goossens was a world-famous conductor and composer, a friend of Picasso and Stravinsky. "My heart just loosens when I listen to Goossens," wrote his pal Noël Coward. In 1947, aged 54 and at the height of his career, he was lured to Australia to take charge of the newly formed Sydney Symphony Orchestra.

The elegant maestro was an instant hit, drawing audiences of 20,000 to free outdoor concerts, introducing Prokofiev to Sydney, mounting a production of his own opera *Judith* with an unknown local stenographer named Joan Sutherland in the title role, and persuading a dubious premier that Sydney needed an opera house and Bennelong Point was its only suitable location. In 1955 he was knighted for services to Australian music. But his fall was coming, soon and sudden.

In 1952, he'd bought a book of artworks by Rosaleen Norton.

'Roie' Norton was a notorious woman. As a child she had a crush on Dracula and a thing for spiders. Expelled from her Chatswood girls' school for being a corrupting influence, she financed her art education by writing horror stories and modelling for Norman Lindsay, who called her "a grubby little girl with great skill". Her paintings, a swirling melange of demons, naked bodies and occult symbolism, were grist for the mill of society's moral guardians and police had raided exhibitions of her work. The press dubbed her the Witch of Kings Cross.

Goossens wrote to Norton and she invited him to tea at her Brougham Street flat, just a short stroll from his office at the ABC. He stayed for the secret rites of Pan.

Unfortunately, Norton's coven had been infiltrated by one of the slithering minions of Beelzebub, a journalist from the *Sun* newspaper. Snooping behind her sofa, the hack discovered a bundle of letters in which Goossens described the bat-wing envelopings and "delicious orificial tingling" of their intimate rituals.

A sting was set in motion. When Goossens went to London for his knightly dubbing, the *Sun* had him followed. Landing back at Mascot, he was met by a posse of police, customs officers and slavering newshounds. In his luggage were "pornographic" pictures, rubber masks and incriminating sticks of incense. The great man's disgrace was total. Convicted of violating the Customs Act, he left the country, never to return.

Rosaleen Norton died in 1979. Witches are now called goths and Eugene Goossens is an auditorium in Ultimo.

WHEN PETER LALOR'S MOMENT IN HIStory arrived, it caught him by surprise. He'd come to Australia to strike it rich, not to lead a rebellion. The 27-year-old Irishman had shown no interest in politics in his native country. A Catholic from a once-prosperous, famine-bankrupted background, he spent his days down a mineshaft, eking gold from the Eureka reef. Joining the Ballarat Reform League was no more than a reaction to the heavy-handed methods of arbitrary officialdom. When 12,000 of his fellow diggers gathered on Bakery Hill in November 1854 to hoist the Southern Cross and burn their licences, Lalor proposed they elect a committee.

At 34, Raffaello Carboni was an experienced rebel. An anti-clerical member of the nationalist movement Young Italy, he'd been wounded in one of the early battles of the Risorgimento. Exiled in London, he had succumbed to gold fever and temporarily forsaken his career as a linguist and writer. Like Lalor, he had been in Australia for just over two years.

Events in Ballarat were moving quickly, drawing in the cautious Irishman. When mounted soldiers charged a group of diggers, open rebellion erupted. In the angry mill of the mob, Peter Lalor mounted a stump, ordered the men into ranks and told them to choose their captains. Carboni stepped forward to offer his services.

Lalor grasped the red-haired Italian's hand and pointed to the non-English-speaking diggers. "I want you, Signore, to tell these gentlemen that if they can't provide themselves with firearms, let each procure a six-inch long piece of steel. Attached to a pole, that'll pierce the tyrant's heart."

When the ranks of diggers formed around the flagstaff and Lalor led them in vowing by the Southern Cross to defend their rights and liberties, Carboni believed he was witnessing something momentous.

The captains gathered to elect a commander-in-chief. Lalor demurred, pleading that he had no military expertise. Carboni's name was put forward, his battle scars cited as evidence of his experience. The Italian insisted that Lalor had a cool head and the confidence of the men. He nominated the Irishman, who was duly elected.

The assault on Eureka cost Lalor his arm and put Carboni in the dock for high treason. But popular sentiment prevailed, and both men were eventually rewarded with public office. Peter Lalor was elected to parliament; Carboni was appointed a local court official. He used the time to pen a pacy chronicle of the rebellion.

Lalor died at 62, an esteemed elder statesman. Carboni returned to Italy, rejoined Garibaldi's campaign, wrote plays and novels, and died in obscurity and poverty aged 55.

Faith Bandler & Paul Robeson

MONEY WAS TIGHT WHEN FAITH BANDLER was growing up in Murwillumbah in the early 1930s, but her two older brothers managed to save a portion of their wages to buy records. Paul Robeson was a favourite and the family would all sing along. At 17, Faith sneaked away from a church meeting to see him perform 'Ol' Man River' in *Showboat*. It was the first movie she ever saw.

Young Faith's interest was more than just musical. The daughter of a South Sea Islander blackbirded to the Queensland canefields, she already saw parallels between the Afro-American experience of segregation and the petty Australian apartheid that distinguished islanders from Aborigines while discriminating against both.

In the person of Paul Robeson, Jim Crow had a particularly formidable opponent. The son of an escaped slave, Robeson had graduated from Columbia Law School and become the greatest American football player of his era before winning worldwide acclaim as an actor and singer. But when he exercised his freedom of speech to oppose racism and fascism, the FBI targeted him. In 1950, the US government revoked his passport and his recordings disappeared from the shelves of American stores.

Faith Bandler found some of his discs in Europe the following year. Now in her early thirties and a peace activist, she'd taken leave from her job as a dressmaker at David Jones in Sydney to attend a Soviet-sponsored youth festival in Berlin. When she returned home, sceptical of the communists, the security police confiscated her passport and her phonograph records, the Robesons among them. They also had her sacked from her job.

After almost a decade, the US Supreme Court restored Robeson's passport. In 1960, he embarked on an overseas concert tour. When he got to Australia, Faith Bandler was at the airport to meet him.

"'You must tell me more about your people,' he said. Well, actually he meant the Aboriginal people …"

She set up a projector in his hotel, the Australia, and screened a film shot on a mission. What he saw moved him to anger and the declaration that he would come back and lend his hand to the struggle for racial equality. "He was beautiful, but he died and he didn't come back."

But his example fuelled Bandler's determination. By the time of Robeson's death, in 1976, she had helped establish the Federal Council for the Advancement of Aborigines and Torres Strait Islanders and led its successful campaign in the 1967 referendum.

And at 90, a Living Treasure, her passion for human rights and social justice jes' keeps rollin' along.

A T 22, HENRY LAWSON WAS DIRT POOR, painfully shy and deaf as a post. His first few poems had garnered considerable praise but writing was "clearly not to be relied on as a means of support". Haphazardly schooled, he found work where he could, mainly as a house painter. The grinding daily slog left him exhausted and frustrated.

His mum, Louisa, had a bright idea. In the political flurry that was Sydney in the 1880s, she'd intersected with the premier, the venerable Sir Henry Parkes. The *Republican*, Louisa's pushy little rag, was in favour of female suffrage. So was Sir Henry. A nod from the top would go a long way towards securing a government position for the promising young bard from Eurunderee. A spot at the railway workshop, say. Henry was qualified, experienced and his references were excellent, so it wasn't a lot to ask. And Parkes had form as a devotee of the muse poetic.

It was 50 years since the pre-eminent figure in colonial politics had arrived in Sydney as an assisted immigrant. Working-class in origin and Chartist in opinion, he was a poet before he was a politician. By the time Louisa Lawson's letter hit his desk, he'd jettisoned his radicalism, grown an enormous white beard, collected a swag of royal honours, won the premiership of New South Wales four times, spent time as a house guest of Tennyson and penned four volumes of unspeakably terrible verse.

He agreed to meet Mrs Lawson's son. But the nervous young Henry undersold himself, both as a tradesman and a poet. And Parkes, much given to oratorical rotundity, was not much impressed with this "gone a-droving" stuff anyway. The "boy" was a mere "improver", he concluded.

The job did not materialise. Looking elsewhere, Lawson went bush, combining journalism with the life of an itinerant labourer. It was thirsty work.

Two months after their meeting, Parkes kick-started federation with a speech at the Tenterfield School of Arts. In it, he proclaimed "with sanguine imminence of morn ... the day of the dominion born".

When that glorious morn eventually dawned, Parkes was five years dead and Lawson had become the most popular writer in the country, a creator of works that spoke the soul of its people. In 1920, he was granted a commonwealth literary pension of a pound a week. But by that stage, he was long past carin'. He died in 1922, a ghost of a man and a martyr to the turps.

On Thursday, 24 December 1914, an athletic young Hawaiian strode across the beach at Freshwater, a stretch of sand between Manly and Curl Curl. The day was clear and sunny, and Duke Kahanamoku was about to perform a feat never before seen in Australia.

Kahanamoku was 25, a Waikiki beach boy whose 'flutter kick' had won him a gold medal for the American team at the 1912 Stockholm Olympics and an invitation from the New South Wales Swimming Association to demonstrate his technique at a meet at the Domain Baths. He was also invited to give a display of 'board-shooting', a novelty which the aquatic-minded Australians were keen to witness. There being no surfboards in the country, Kahanamoku constructed one from a solid plank of local sugar pine.

By the time he entered the water a sizeable crowd had gathered, including a local schoolgirl and avid ocean swimmer, Isabel Letham. Rapidly outpacing his escort of lifesavers, Kahanamoku paddled through the breakers, sat on his board in the calm beyond the surf line and awaited a suitable wave. When it came, he swung the board around and glided all the way to the shore, kneeling at first, then standing. It was, the *Sydney Morning Herald* reported the next day, "wonderfully clever". When Kahanamoku called for a volunteer to help demonstrate tandem surfing, Letham was first in line.

The bronzed Hawaiian with the mane of black hair and full-sail shoulders made it seem easy, but when the 15-year-old Australian looked down from the crest into the trough, she thought she was "going over a cliff". For three waves she resisted Kahanamoku's attempts to get her upright. Finally, he yanked her to her feet. After that, she was "hooked for life". When Duke Kahanamoku returned to Sydney after competing in a slate of eastern-state swim meets, Isabel Letham rode with him at Dee Why, amid considerable publicity.

Australia had a new enthusiasm and its first surfer had an international profile. Fearless, forthright and glamorous, Letham headed to America. San Francisco appointed her its director of swimming, but the Manly Surf Club's refusal to grant membership to a woman left Letham without credentials as a lifesaver and stymied her attempt to establish Australian-style lifesaving clubs there. She returned home to teach water ballet. When she died, in 1995, her ashes were consigned to the waves by a circle of board riders.

Duke Kahanamoku is remembered as the Big Kahuna, the father of modern surfing. His original board has pride of place in the Freshwater Surf Lifesaving Club.

WILFRED BURCHETT WAS A TAD WARY when he presented his ID to the sentry at the White House on a foggy morning in October 1971. His passport was Cuban and his UN press pass restricted him to New York. But the marine waved him through and, sure enough, President Nixon's national security adviser was waiting in the West Wing to greet him.

Burchett reported on wars, making little effort to hide his partisan sympathies. Henry Kissinger made wars, unfussed by notions of neutrality or civilian casualties. Both traded in information and knew their way around the back channels. The peace talks in Paris had stalled and Kissinger wanted to know what the Australian journalist's friends in the North Vietnamese politburo were thinking.

At first sight, the smiling Kissinger reminded Burchett of an indulgent headmaster from his school days. Breakfast was served and terms agreed. The conversation was to be off the record, but Kissinger would not be heartbroken if the fact of their meeting became known.

To begin, like two dogs circling each other, they discussed China, sharing their mutual admiration for Zhou Enlai. The subject soon shifted to the negotiations in Paris. Kissinger probed Burchett on the top personalities in the Hanoi leadership. He was frustrated by the intransigence of the Reds. They were unwilling to be bombed into allowing the Americans to set their own departure timetable. Their language was insufficiently deferential. Their peace plan was "a bore".

Burchett, as tubby and bespectacled as his host, had just spent six months crawling through Vietcong tunnels, witnessing firsthand the effects of American air power. He countered that being stuck with the corrupt Saigon regime must have been an even bigger bore. The coldness of Kissinger's eyes, he noted, belied the warmth of his smile.

The phone rang. It was Nixon, fine-tuning a communiqué announcing a presidential visit to the Soviet Union. Talk then circled back to China, where Kissinger was enmeshed in secret negotiations that would shortly lead to its recognition by the US.

Returning to New York, Burchett got word that Kissinger considered their chat "fruitful". It was not Burchett's insights he valued, however, so much as the hope their meeting would be read in Hanoi as a signal that America's intention to withdraw was genuine. For his part, Burchett got a scoop on Nixon's forthcoming trip to Moscow.

After decades of vilification in his native land, Wilfred Burchett died in Bulgaria in 1983. His ghost still haunts the concentric trenches of Australian academia. The innumerable crimes of Henry Kissinger remain unpunished.

Paul Strzelecki had itchy feet. The son of a minor nobleman, without land or title, he quit Poland aged 33 and headed for England. There, he pursued geology and began to style himself as count.

Then it was Africa, then Canada and the US, Mexico and Cuba. Charm opened doors and rare rocks paid the bills. Strzelecki hiked most of the way, the better to study the terrain and spot minerals. In 1836, he walked from Chile to California. In Hawaii, he climbed a volcano. In June 1839, he dined at Government House in Sydney.

Present at the meal was Lady Jane Franklin, wife of the lieutenant-governor of Van Diemen's Land and vigorous supporter of antipodean science. She'd once had a thing for Peter Mark Roget, inventor of the thesaurus, but married a naval officer and explorer when her affections were unrequited, abnegated, rejected, spurned. Franklin was knighted soon after their marriage and some saw her Ladyship as the brains of the partnership.

Lady Jane took an immediate shine to the "most agreeable Pole". No slouch herself in the gadabout department, she had trekked overland from Melbourne shortly before, the first white woman to do so. Conversation possibly touched upon the Illawarra, a promising source of fossils. In any case, they "talked much".

Strzelecki began to prepare an expedition. After calling again on Lady Jane, he made a 2000-mile circuit of New South Wales. Declaring the mineralogy "very tame", he then marched south to conduct a more general geographical survey. On 12 March 1840, after a supper of lyrebird, he hauled his instruments to the top of a craggy protuberance that reminded him of Poland's national hero.

He spent the next two years in Tasmania as a guest of Lady Jane and Sir John, travelling extensively, conducting experiments, making maps and writing up his notes. Lady Jane was also busy furthering the cause of science by being lugged to Macquarie Harbour by a team of convicts.

Helped by a hefty donation from his scientific friends in Tasmania, Strzelecki returned to England in 1843 to publish his findings. He became a naturalised British subject and a luminary of the Royal Geographical Society. Lady Jane, meanwhile, was financing search parties for her husband who had perished, with his entire crew, in an attempt to find the North-West Passage.

Strzelecki is now a highway between Mirboo North and Leongatha. The *Lady Jane Franklin* is a fast, quiet, spacious and environmentally designed cruise ship.

On 1 December 1945, as British rule of India entered its tumultuous final phase, Mohandas Gandhi arrived in Calcutta. That night, he held the first of a series of meetings with the raj's local representative, Richard Casey, the governor of Bengal.

Dick Casey was an Australian, a Cambridge-educated scion of the Queensland squattocracy. Treasurer in the conservative Lyons government, he'd run against Menzies for party leadership. In one of his first acts as prime minister, Menzies made Casey ambassador to Washington, effectively removing him from domestic politics for the duration of the war.

After Washington, Casey went to Cairo as British minister of state, a move that did not play well with the new Curtin government at home. When Churchill offered him the post in Calcutta, complete with a peerage, Casey accepted the job but not the title. With hopes of a political future back in Australia still alive, he thought a title would "much reduce my chances in my very democratic country".

He found Bengal bruised by communal rioting, riven by nationalist agitation and devastated by a man-made famine that had left 3 million dead. And his nationality didn't make his role any easier. Being ruled by a Brit was bad enough, but taking orders from a colonial Brit from a country built on racial discrimination was downright insulting.

Afflicted with boils and amoebic dysentery, and sharing his immense, run-down official residence with hundreds of servants, their extended families and various species of uninvited wildlife, Casey was appalled by the crude racism of the British elite. To the chagrin of the local *memsahibs*, he began entertaining on a lavish scale, with a high proportion of Indian guests.

By the time the *mahatma* arrived – just two months before Casey's tenure expired – the imperial Australian had earned a reputation as a vigorous, pragmatic and even-handed administrator. Casey thought Gandhi "lively" for a man of 76, with "a good sense of humour". But the future of the subcontinent was no joking matter. After a long talk, further discussions were scheduled. As Casey escorted Gandhi to his car through the long corridors of Government House, hundreds of servants emerged to watch their progress – Hindus, Muslims and others, each making "his customary salute".

The two men continued to meet and correspond warmly, but Casey's appointment was winding down. In January, he shot a tiger. In February, he headed back to Australia. Eventually, after serving as minister for external affairs throughout the 1950s, he got his peerage. In 1965, as Baron Casey of Berwick, he became governor-general. By then, many of Gandhi's fears of a divided India had been realised.

THEY WERE NEW CHUMS, FRESH OFF THE boat. Daisy May O'Dwyer was 20, the porcelain-skinned daughter of a drunkard doctor from Cashel. Edwin Henry Murrant, a year younger, was English and claimed to be the illegitimate son of an admiral. For each, Australia was a blank slate, a chance to invent themselves.

Daisy was, by her own description, "passionate". She was also hard-headed, a woman without means or prospects in a man's world. Edwin, as well as being handsome and gallant, had the whiff of a pedigree and prospects of a remittance.

Their paths crossed at Fanning Downs Station, near Charters Towers. He was a groom, a skilful and daring horseman. She, orphanage educated but well connected, was employed as the governess. After a lightning courtship, they tied the knot on 13 March 1884.

It took less than a month to unravel. Murrant first dudded the clergyman of his honorarium, then bought a saddle and a pair of horses with a dud cheque and took off for the lights of Cloncurry. On the way, he was busted. The charge sheet included the theft of 32 pigs.

Daisy didn't post bail or attend the trial. Clearly, her dashing young groom was no gentleman. Nor was he any longer a Murrant. The name he signed on the bogus cheque was Harry Morant. He was still using it

18 years later, when he was executed in Pretoria for the murder of unarmed prisoners. By then, he was also known as 'the Breaker', a penner of bush ballads for the *Bulletin*.

Undeterred by the brevity of her first marriage, Daisy promptly entered into another, albeit bigamously. As Mrs Bates, she bore a child, before ditching matrimony to flit back to Britain, where she dabbled in journalism. Commissioned by a London paper to report on atrocities against Aborigines, she returned to Australia shortly before Morant embarked for the war in South Africa.

While the Breaker was riding the veldt, doing the Empire's dirty work, Daisy Bates was beginning her lifelong journey into Australian mythology. Disguised as Mary Poppins, complete with furled umbrella, she spent the next 40 years observing, documenting and interpreting traditional Aboriginal customs, "to make their passing easy". As 'Kabbarli' – the grandmother – the self-taught anthropologist and serial bigamist took a censorious view of the morals of the natives. Infanticide and cannibalism were apparently not beyond them.

As far as is known, all contact between the pair ended with their marriage. Bates burned her voluminous notes before her death. And Morant must have had another in mind when he penned 'Love Outlasteth All'. A horse, possibly.

ALFRED DEAKIN OCCUPIED MANY NOTABLE posts and earned several memorable sobriquets in his long and distinguished public career. Member for Ballarat, minister for public works and water supply, chief secretary and solicitor-general of Victoria, executive chairman of the Federation League, first attorney-general of the Commonwealth of Australia, prime minister three times. Affable Alfred, Father of Irrigation.

An omnivorous reader and assiduous writer, Deakin filled an endless stream of notebooks and diaries, subsisted for a time as a journalist, contributed 'secret' commentary on Australian politics to the London press, published a five-act blank-verse drama on the Renaissance-era Flemish painter of grotesques Quentin Massys, and penned essays, poetry and treatises on subjects as diverse as funerary architecture in India and anti-sweating legislation. But his most intriguing work of literature was composed at the very beginning of his career when, barely 22, he occupied his first office: president of the Victorian Association of Progressive Spiritualists.

Spiritualism was enjoying a certain vogue by the 1870s, and young Alfred's search for a Higher Truth drew him to its mystic endeavours. At séances conducted by his psychic mentor, a former draper, he proved an ideal medium. In short order, he was communicating with the disincarnate departed. And not just any passing apparition. Deakin found himself taking post-mortem dictation from the shade of John Bunyan, the nonconformist poet whose bodily departure from this mortal coil occurred in the distant year of 1688.

A contemporary of Milton, Bunyan was an uneducated tinker who did most of his writing in jail, where he was banged up for more than 12 years for preaching without a permit. His allegory *The Pilgrim's Progress* was once one of the most widely read books in English literature, as familiar to many Protestants as the Bible itself.

In the original version, published in 1678, Christian, its everyman protagonist, undertakes a perilous journey to Heaven, overcoming the temptations of Madam Wanton and Vanity Fair, escaping Doubting Castle and the Slough of Despond, before arriving at the Celestial City, thereby assuring a pre-eminent place in the Glossary of Phrases Proverbial.

As channelled through Alfred Deakin, two centuries later, *A New Pilgrim's Progress* featured a hero named Restless, who found his true path via vegetarianism. It was published pseudonymously, crediting Bunyan with spiritual guidance. Shortly after, Deakin began his political career by running for parliament. Denounced in the papers for "outraging religion", he withdrew from the spiritualist movement.

Alfred Deakin died in 1919, a spent force politically, his mystical questions unanswered. He is also known as a Founding Father of the Liberal Party.

As a small child growing up in Melbourne, Percy Grainger devoured the Icelandic sagas, signed his letters "Grettir the Strong" and bounded up every available stairway. His adoring mother Rose, meanwhile, was showing him what happens to naughty boys who neglect their piano practice. In 1894, aged 12, Percy made his concert debut. The *Argus* declared him a remarkable instance of juvenile precocity. Rose promptly relocated him to Europe.

In London in 1906, he met Edvard Grieg at a high-society dinner. The celebrated Norwegian composer was a physical wreck. Plagued with pleurisy, arthritis and nocturnal hallucinations, the 63-year-old was charmed at energetic young Percy's enthusiasm for some of his lesser-known pieces. After hearing him play, the master of trollish anthems and Nordic maunderings declared Grainger "a genius that we Scandinavians cannot do other than love". Grainger, likewise, was enthralled. Already in search of folkloric inspiration, he considered Grieg an iconoclast with an "elvish sparkle".

The following summer, the two musicians spent a week together at the Scandinavian maestro's home in Troldhaugen, intensively rehearsing Grieg's piano concerto. A performance was scheduled for October in Leeds, with Grieg to conduct.

But the tiny, enervated Norseman was on his last legs. An unsuccessful Finsen Electric Light Bath treatment had failed to cure his insomnia, breathlessness and terrible nightmares. On the day before his departure for England, his heart gave out under the strain.

Although they had known each other for just 15 months, Grainger continued to champion Grieg's work until his own death, in 1961. By then, Percy had moved permanently to the United States, where the Duo-Art piano-roll sales of his 'Country Gardens' enabled him to indulge in some of his more flamboyant interests. These included propounding the superiority of the Nordic races, inventing a 'blue-eyed' language free of Latinate impurities, designing towelling clothing and satisfying a lifelong taste for flagellation.

The composer of hundreds of pieces of music and a virtuoso performer in thousands of concerts, Percy Grainger left a large musical legacy, a sizeable collection of custom-made whips, his dental X-rays and an experimental music machine called the Kangaroo Pouch. Edvard Grieg got a day of national mourning. His 'Morning Mood' will be instantly recognisable to Looney Tunes fans.

WHEN LABOR WON THE 1983 ELECTION, David Combe thought he had it made. As ALP national secretary he'd put the party apparatus on a professional footing, secured its finances and paved the way for Bob Hawke's eventual victory. Now a commercial lobbyist, the lifetime Labor insider was to be the indispensable go-to man for corporations wanting to do business with the new government.

Quick to congratulate him was the first secretary at the Soviet embassy. At 31, Valery Ivanov was young for the job, his first diplomatic posting. The homesick Muscovite arrived at Combe's house on the day after the election bearing champagne and cigars.

The two men had met a year earlier at an Australia–USSR Friendship Society cocktail party at the Canberra Labor Club. Combe was a prominent member of the society, alert to lucrative trade prospects with Russia. Ivanov was working his diplomatic beat. Over the following months, the stiff, humourless envoy began assiduously to cultivate the Billy Bunterish would-be entrepreneur.

All the while, ASIO was watching. A high-level Soviet defector to Britain had fingered Ivanov as KGB. To the guardians of national security, long lacking a public triumph, the lobbyist was bait to catch a spy. Unknowingly, Combe was riding for a fall.

If Combe guessed Ivanov's true role, he wasn't much fussed. His business was influence, not intelligence. He had no secrets, and his Labor friends were in power. Theirs was a business relationship, open and above board.

Two weeks into Hawke's tenure, the nation's secret-police chief advised the new PM that one of his old mates was being cultivated by a foreign power. "Classic" signs of "disinformation" and "clandestinity" had been detected. Hidden microphones had recorded Combe explaining the term "jobs for the boys". Tellingly, he was known to be "anti-American".

Without further ado, Combe was hung out to dry, denied access, cold-shouldered. Ivanov was expelled. In the ensuing brouhaha, a royal commission was called. After months of testimony, it cleared Combe, absolved the government and exonerated ASIO.

His livelihood in tatters, Combe was eventually eased into the post of Australian trade commissioner in Vancouver. After that, he became an international wine consultant.

Of Ivanov, less is known. The surname is not uncommon. The KGB is officially defunct and its former members are difficult to trace. But a certain Valery Ivanov serves on the Standing Committee for Foreign Affairs and National Security of the Republic of Belarus. He looks older, of course, but the physical similarity is unmistakable. And the job seems tailor-made for one of the boys.

His true name is nowhere recorded, nor his date of birth. Born in the Hunter Valley around 1833, he was known to his white employer simply as Jackey Jackey. A clever and skilful lad, he was recommended to Edmund Kennedy, an assistant surveyor of Crown lands.

Kennedy had arrived in the colony in 1840 with "an almost mad ambition to distinguish himself". So far, he'd served on Mitchell's expeditions in central and western Queensland and established himself in Sydney society as a charming bachelor with a good singing voice. In 1848, not yet 30, he was given command of an expedition to explore the Cape York Peninsula. He landed in May, near what is now Mission Beach, with 27 horses, 250 sheep, three wooden carts, four convicts, a taxidermist, a botanist, four ex-convicts and Jackey Jackey.

It took two months to cover 20 miles. Ill and exhausted, the party was kept moving only by the inspiring leadership of Kennedy and the bushcraft of Jackey Jackey. A strong rapport developed between the two and when Kennedy decided to leave the bulk of the group behind and strike north for the waiting relief ship, he took Jackey Jackey with him.

The peoples of the Cape York 'sandbeach' country had a long history of contact with other races. Of their five main language groups, the most warlike was the 'cruel' Yadhaykenu. As Kennedy and Jackey Jackey thrashed through the flooded, croc-infested tributaries of the Escape River, Yadhaykenu warriors closed around them. Kennedy hoped they were friendly. Their barbed spears and muttering convinced Jackey Jackey otherwise. "Those blackfellows, they too much speak," he told the boss.

A hail of spears felled the horses and skewered Kennedy through the back and thigh. Jackey Jackey managed to get off a round of buckshot, but Kennedy's powder was wet and his gun misfired. Fatally wounded, he entrusted his notes and maps to his companion, fell back into his arms and died. Still under sustained attack, JJ hastily buried Kennedy, hid his papers and escaped through the rain. Lionised in Sydney, he was presented with a silver breastplate and a £50 bank account. An admiring public plied him with "ardent spirits".

'Jackey Jackey' entered the vernacular. For whites it was a generic dismissive, denying blacks their individuality and hence their dignity. To blacks it meant a collaborator, the subservient native complicit in his own people's dispossession.

Jackey Jackey died after falling, drunk, into a campfire. He'd never worn his breastplate and his untouched reward money reverted to consolidated revenue. In the 50 years following Kennedy's expedition, the Indigenous population of Cape York fell from 3000 to 100. Their descendants welcome tourists.

I N 1935 TO BE CATHOLIC WAS TO BE IRISH, AND the hierarchy ruled its flock with a firm doctrinal hand and an unchallenged tribal authority – no one more so than Daniel Mannix, the venerable Cork-born archbishop of Melbourne. Tall, gaunt and magisterial, Mannix was already ancient. Born in 1864, he had become a contentious ecclesiastical figure in the Irish nationalist movement. Shipped to Australia, his stand against conscription led to demands for his deportation. In 1920, the Royal Navy prevented him landing in his insurgent homeland and he returned to Australia, reviled by the Protestant establishment and revered by his spiritual constituents.

A pious Catholic, Bob Santamaria was no son of Erin. The energetic and ambitious child of an Italian greengrocer, he'd worked long hours in the family fruit shop in Brunswick, won a place at university and joined the Campion Society, a lay organisation dedicated to the study of papal encyclicals and social theory. At 20, he was already convinced that he was an agent of the Almighty, "forehead marked with sign of Cross", chosen to stem the tide of secular materialism that threatened to derail God's plan for the world. To begin his mission, he needed the archbishop's imprimatur for a new weekly publication, the *Catholic Worker*.

Fifty years his senior and the former head of a seminary, Mannix had doubtless encountered many zealous young men. For almost two hours he meandered, leading the discussion over topics as diverse as the war in Abyssinia and the policies of Roosevelt, until Santamaria began to think he was getting the brush-off. As Mannix rose to end the interview, Santamaria restated his request. Did he have His Grace's permission to establish a Catholic paper? You don't need it, Mannix replied, extending his hand with "an unexpectedly firm grasp".

On that handshake was sealed an alliance that did not falter until Mannix's death, 28 years later. Appointed soon after to run Catholic Action, Santamaria left the prelate's mansion, Raheen, "jumping for joy". Using the authority of the church and the methods of the communists to fight a secretive war in the unions, he engineered a split that kept Labor out of power for decades. When the Vatican condemned Santamaria's "Movement" as theologically unsound, Mannix declared him "the saviour of Australia".

Aged 99, Mannix collapsed on Cup Day 1963 and died the next day, Santamaria at his bedside. They had just learned that DLP preferences to the Liberals had secured state aid for Catholic schools. Eventually outliving communism, Santamaria turned his apocalyptic ire on capitalism, winning him pre-posthumous rehabilitation by some of his old enemies before his death in 1998.

MARTHA GELLHORN WROTE MANY things during her remarkable 60-year career. Reports on living conditions in the mine and mill towns of Depression-era America. Newspaper despatches from battlefronts as far-flung as Spain, Finland, Java and El Salvador. Trenchant and prophetic observations on the rise of fascism. Eyewitness accounts of wars, insurrections, revolutions and invasions. Novels, collections of short stories, travelogues and autobiography.

In 1975, she wrote a 'fan letter' to a stranger she saw on television. He was a 35-year-old Australian journalist named John Pilger. Gellhorn had chanced upon an interview in which Pilger was copping a mauling for his first book, *The Last Day*, an eyewitness account of the hasty American retreat from Saigon. Personally acquainted with the reception often given to the bearers of unpalatable news, she promptly went out and bought the book. Judging it fine, she wrote to Pilger to tell him so.

Pilger, it transpired, owed his introduction to Indochina to Gellhorn. Eight years earlier, her articles on the horrors being unleashed on Vietnam's civilians had prompted Pilger's editor at the *Daily Mirror* to send him to cover the war. Pilger found Gellhorn's fan mail "moving", but it was another three years before the two inveterate travellers were to meet.

In 1978, following the screening of Pilger's documentary *Do You Remember Vietnam?*, they finally sat down together.

Gellhorn kept a flat, a court of sorts, in London's Cadogan Square. As a young Midwesterner in Paris, she'd modelled for Chanel and Schiaparelli, and she retained a slim, striking elegance that must have contrasted to the lanky Aussie with fiercely independent hair. Over a bottle of Famous Grouse, they talked about "the struggle of memory against organised forgetting", agreeing furiously on almost everything. The exception was Palestine. Gellhorn was one of the first journalists to enter Dachau and her adherence to Israel was unqualified. Pilger steered around the subject and the two became good friends.

Strongly averse to "the kitchen of life", the former Mrs Ernest Hemingway was a terrible cook. On subsequent visits, Pilger took food. Sometimes they would stroll in the park, talking surfing and snorkelling between denouncing the vileness of Kissinger. An incorrigible smoker, Gellhorn once got them thrown out of Selfridges for lighting up.

Martha Gellhorn was still reporting in her eighties, travelling to Panama in the wake of the American invasion and interviewing street kids in the favelas of Brazil. She died of cancer in 1998. John Pilger continues to annoy the buggery out of his critics.

In the 40 years since young Redmond Barry's arrival in Melbourne, low on cash and prospects, the raw frontier town of 5000 souls had grown into a grand and well-appointed metropolis. And the ambitious Irish barrister had played no small part in its progress. Its library, university, art gallery and museum were the result of his tireless and conscientious exertions. Cultured, courteous, liberal enough to cohabit openly with his mistress and give their four children his name, Barry could take pride in the civilisation he had nurtured in the antipodean wilderness.

But beyond the reaches of the city, untamed and lawless elements saw fit to wage war against the agents of that civilisation. And in his capacity as chief justice of Victoria, it often fell upon Sir Redmond Barry KCMG to bring these feral elements to book. In 1876, he had no compunction in sending an indigent middle-aged woman to prison for three years for conspiring with her horse-thief sons. And now, four years later, one of those sons was standing before him in the dock to receive due retribution for the cold-blooded murder of a police constable.

In the three months since his capture at Glenrowan, Ned Kelly's gunshot wounds had begun to heal. His sense of injustice, however, was still red-raw. A fair trial, the notorious bushranger hoped, would show that he had acted in self-defence. The police had come hunting him with intent to kill, and he acted under strong provocation. But his lawyer called no witnesses and argued legal technicalities. It took the jury only 25 minutes to find the defendant guilty.

Kelly heard the verdict in silence. Asked if he had anything to say before being sentenced, he leaned on the dock and began to speak, his voice low but clearly audible. Neither his lawyers nor the jury were to blame, he said. He should have spoken up when he had the chance – but that would have looked like flashness.

Barry cleared his throat and began to pronounce sentence. But Kelly cut him short. The Crown would have been better served, he said, had the court allowed him to examine the witnesses. It would've made no difference, countered Barry. Back and forth, the unschooled bushman and the erudite judge traded points, neither persuading the other. "Edward Kelly," concluded Barry, "I hereby sentence you to death by hanging."

"I will see you there where I go," replied Kelly.

Twelve days after Kelly's execution, Barry dropped dead from congested lungs and a carbuncle on the neck. Kelly left a legend. Barry left almost nothing. He'd given his money, anonymously, to the worthy poor. Such is life.

IN EARLY 1882, SHANE MALONEY WENT scouting for a graphic designer. As public-relations officer of the Boy Scouts Association, he was responsible for production of the organisation's annual report. New to the PR game, he needed somebody to show him the ropes. Following the wail of a plaintive mouth-organ along St Kilda Road, he found himself in the studio of an advertising art director named Chris Grosz. Strangely, the harmonica-playing ad-man did not have a ponytail. There was, nevertheless, something eerily familiar about him.

Grosz, a Dunedin-born tussock-grubber and hay-baler, had fled to Australia in the late 1970s to escape allegations of nib-filching during a stint as cartoonist at the *Christchurch Star*. Moving from job to job in a vain attempt to elude his creditors, he'd eventually found work designing tour posters for a small firm of ethnically stereotypical rock entrepreneurs. Coincidentally, Maloney was employed by the same organisation in the same rat-infested, closet-sized office at exactly the same time as Grosz, although he claims to have no recollection of the then-hirsute Kiwi illustrator. This he attributes to "drugs" and the pressures of a job selling no-talent guitar bands to till-skimming venue operators.

Grosz lavished the full panoply of his skills on the Scout Association report. Unfortunately, his enthu-siasm for woggles raised eyebrows within the organisation's higher echelons. Soon after, Maloney was compelled to relinquish his lemon-squeezer and seek employment elsewhere.

By then, Grosz, too, had folded his tent. He moved first to Greece where he lived rent-free in the house of a pipe-puffing Dutch-born film director, then to Bali where he concentrated on painting and bludging. On his return to Australia, he discovered that Maloney was skippering the new Melbourne Comedy Festival. After several attempts, he ingratiated himself suffi-ciently to be invited to preside over an exhibition of New Zealand political cartoonists, all more famous and talented than him.

Twenty years later, Maloney again approached him. Now a minor crime novelist, bloated with self-impor-tance, Maloney had conned a fly-by-night magazine into paying top dollar for a regular feature based on a half-baked idea that would only work if it was daubed with multi-coloured scribbles.

By then, Grosz was back in the country of his birth, pursuing his lifelong interests in sheep obstetrics and lawn maintenance. Reluctantly, and only because he "needs the money", he agreed to join Maloney in the creation of *Australian Encounters*. The rest is what passes for history.